Breakthrough Prayers,
Decrees and
Confessions

Published by VJ Alston International Ministries
10936 North Port Washington Road, Suite 226
Mequon, Wisconsin 53092
drvjalston.org

Printed in the United States of America

ISBN 978-0-9908585-2-2

Design Director: Venner J. Alston
Cover Design by David Guillen Velasco
Interior Design by Monica Barros Gomes Silva

BREAKTHROUGH PRAYERS,
DECREES AND CONFESSIONS

OVERCOMING
DEMONIC RESISTANCE
THROUGH
WARFARE PRAYER

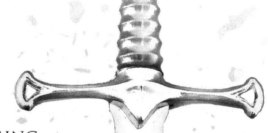

VENNER J. ALSTON

CONTENTS

INTRODUCTION

I was on my way to services in my church when the phone rang. It was a friend whose daughter had suffered from major pregnancy complications that several times resulted in the loss of her children. Her current pregnancy had been going well until two days before she was scheduled to deliver. When she awakened, she realized her unborn baby was not moving, and she could not find a heartbeat. She told her mother, who instructed her to go to the emergency room. That was when I received the prayer request from my friend on behalf of her daughter. When I arrived at the services, I shared the situation with the congregation, and we entered into corporate prayer.

This was not prayer as usual. A child's life hung in the balance, and we could not pray in our normal, devotional prayer way. We needed to bombard the heavens with strength and militancy. I understood the magnitude of power we could release in the corporate setting as we came into agreement. *"You'll chase out your enemies and defeat them: Five of you will chase a hundred, and a hundred of you will chase ten thousand and do away with them"* (Leviticus 26:7–8 message). We came into agreement with the parents and the Lord that the baby would live and not die. We purposed to release in the earth what had already been released in heaven. I knew it was the will of the Lord for the child to live and that the assignment of death had to be defeated in prayer.

As we commanded spirits of death and destruction to leave, I called the child into the earth realm. I felt like a general in military service, mobilizing troops and surrounding the enemy.

Our words came crashing into the spiritual realm like a battering ram. We laid siege to the assignment of death that was trying to steal the life of the child. As we prayed, we were focused in the Spirit—one voice, one people, purposed to rebuke death and command life. We were determined not to relent in prayer until we knew our assignment was completed. Suddenly, I heard the Lord tell me to tell the baby to cry. As I decreed, "Cry, baby, cry!" I felt the peace of God come into the room. I knew that all would be well, and the child would be born healthy. An hour later, I received a text message telling me the doctors had found a heartbeat and were preparing to deliver the child. After the delivery, the grandmother reported that not only was the child born at a healthy weight, the child was born crying and cried for ten minutes.

This is how we war in prayer. As the Lord directs us in prayer, we declare His words into the atmosphere. Then every demonic assignment in operation must break. Spiritual warfare prayer is strong, militant prayer. The strength of spiritual warfare is not in volume but in faith. I have seen some believers focus on screaming, yelling, balling up their fists and shaking them in the atmosphere. Emotionalism is not spiritual warfare. The enemy will not bow because you scream, yell or shake your fist. The enemy bows before your faith and your resolve to not relent until the promise of God manifests. He bows before your Kingdom authority, which is expressed as you declare the Word of the Lord revealed in the Scriptures. Jesus used the Word of God to defeat the enemy. Those who will be successful in spiritual warfare must learn how to war in faith using the Word of God.

The book in your hands holds prayers strong enough to tear down the defenses of hell. As a companion to *Next-Level Spiritual Warfare: Advanced Strategies for Defeating the Enemy*, it is meant to encourage those who long to pray more effectively. Spiritual warfare is an integral and inevitable part of every Christian's life. As you increase in biblical wisdom and understanding, so does your capacity to pray effectively and overcome powers of darkness.

Even as we approach the next great awakening, God is positioning the Church to wage effective warfare against the powers of darkness and win. The more we gain more revelation concerning our weapons of warfare and how those powers operate against us, the more effectively we push back the darkness seated in the gates of our cities and nations. In this way, we replace darkness with righteousness.

If you are unfamiliar with this kind of warfare, you might be wondering how to use the prayers in this book. In part 1, the prayers, decrees and confessions are topically arranged; you can view them as targeted engagement against the enemy. Part 2 contains prayers you can use at certain periods of the day, called "watches" in Scripture. Here are some simple steps to help you effectively war in prayer using the prayers in this book:

01. Start by reading *Next-Level Spiritual Warfare: Advanced Strategies for Defeating the Enemy*. Understanding the principles set forth in that book will help you to war more effectively.

02. Find the prayers in this book that most effectively address your situation and refer to them regularly.

03. Pray them aloud. Words have creativity woven into them. Each time you pray or make a declaration or prophetic decree, you are releasing the power of God's Word into the atmosphere. Remember, Jesus said, "If you have faith, you can *say* to this mountain, 'Be removed and be cast into the sea'" (see Matthew 17:20 and Mark 11:23).

04. Be consistent. Find time each day to release prayers, confessions and prophetic decrees.

05. We can pray at any time; praying through the watches, however, is like releasing an arrow that finds its mark at a specific hour of the day, and it is effective. The prayer watches are effective whether you are watching at home or with a group during a corporate gathering.

06. Pray in faith, trusting God to respond.

Let me share one more testimony. I received a prayer request from a family whose daughter had been missing for months. I assured the parents that I would pray; I trusted that if she was alive but unseen, someone would see her, and if she was no longer in the earth, her remains would be found. I mobilized a team of intercessors, and we began to command every occult power that was covering her to be removed. We called her name and commanded her to come into sight from a place of hiddenness. Daily we commanded that she be revealed in the earth. We decreed that she would not remain unseen. We commanded every demonic cloud covering her to dissipate. We partnered with heaven, asking for the angelic host to roll away the stones covering the caves of hiddenness that were imprisoning her.

After two weeks of praying, one of the intercessors was driving home and saw the daughter. She pulled her car over and informed the young woman of our prayers to find her. Some prayer assignments unfold over time. As you are faithful to press in, God will respond.

> *For although we live in the natural realm, we don't wage a military campaign employing human weapons, using manipulation to achieve our aims. Instead, our spiritual weapons are energized with divine power to effectively dismantle the defenses behind which people hide. We can demolish every deceptive fantasy that opposes God and break through every arrogant attitude that is raised up in defiance of the true knowledge of God. We capture, like prisoners of war, every thought and insist that it bow in obedience to the Anointed One.*
>
> **2 CORINTHIANS 10:3–5 PASSION**

PART I
TARGETED
ENGAGEMENT

1. PRAYING THE BLOOD OF JESUS

We are completely free to enter the Most Holy Place. We can do this without fear because of the blood sacrifice of Jesus. We enter through a new way that Jesus opened for us.

HEBREWS 10:19 ERV

I target every assignment of busyness that keeps me from building the altar of prayer. I purpose to spend time in prayer each day.

Prayer is my access of communion and fellowship with my heavenly Father. Today I choose to walk with Him in communion and fellowship, as Adam did.

The power to overcome is in the blood of Jesus and the indwelling of Holy Spirit. I will develop consistent times for prayer so that I experience all that Jesus paid for.

Lord, I thank You for the blood of Jesus that cleanses me from all sin and unrighteousness.

I plead the blood of Jesus over a spirit of careless prayerlessness, in the name of Jesus. I refuse to live a prayerless life.

I am free through the blood of Jesus, for whomever the Son of man sets free is really free!

I plead the blood of Jesus over every assignment that comes against my mind, preventing me from being focused on eternity, in the name of Jesus.

Today I remind the enemy of the power of the blood of Jesus, and I command every assignment set against me to fail.

I decree the authority of the blood of Jesus over every evil assignment delaying my provision, in Jesus' name.

I decree the authority of the blood of Jesus over assignments hindering my progress. Today I begin to progress in a new way. There is a new momentum being released over me right now. I am becoming unstoppable by the power of Holy Spirit.

Today the horn of His salvation is pouring out anointing on me. I plead the blood of Jesus against every spirit keeping me in a low place, and I decree that I am rising in a new way.

Through the blood of Jesus, I have life. Any sickness that is trying to attack my life or the lives of my family members must let go.

Thank You, Father, for the provision of the blood of Jesus.

I command every work of darkness lurking around my life to dry up to the roots by the power of the blood of Jesus.

I plead the blood of Jesus against every assignment of failure at the edge of my miracle. Every assignment of "almost" at the point of breakthrough to keep me from fully breaking through is cast down now, in Jesus' name.

I decree that because I walk in the light and have been cleansed by the blood of Jesus, I have been redeemed out of the hand of the enemy.

Through the blood of Jesus, I am justified, sanctified and made holy.

The power of the cross and the blood of Jesus stand between me and every dark power that would try to operate against me.

My faith is activated in a new way. I have been cleansed by the blood of Jesus.

I receive fresh oil on my life today. My life is soaked with anointing, making me slippery in the hands of the enemy. The powers of hell will not hold me today.

2. EMPOWERED BY THE BLOOD

I am strengthened by the joy of the Lord. I decree that His right hand of righteousness upholds me.

The countenance of the Lord brightens my life. The power of depression and sadness is broken off me. I command the spirit of misery to leave my life now.

I will not fall into the snare of my enemies today. Every pit that has been dug for me, my enemies will fall into.

I decree that I will not be a worshiper only in the corporate gathering. Beginning today, I become a secret worshiper.

Every assignment of hell that has come after my worship life is defeated today. There is no disagreement between my private life of worship and my public life.

Every assignment of spiritual dryness, dullness of hearing and hardness of heart is broken from my life today.

Every demonic assignment that comes to frustrate and hinder my destiny is cast down now.

I decree what is written in Psalm 72, that God is judging my oppressors. Today God is breaking my oppressors in pieces.

I decree that my enemies bow and lick the dust, in Jesus' name!

Let every door that I opened to the enemy be closed now, in the name of Jesus.

Let every wound in my soul be healed, in the name of Jesus.

Every assignment set against my destiny and my purpose is canceled today.

By the power of my words and faith, I set my day and night in Kingdom order. Creation cooperates with me and not against me. Blessings come to me and not curses. Life comes to me and not death.

I receive the virtues, strength, power, might and anointing in the blood of Jesus. Today the blood quickens within me every godly assignment that has died. Let Kingdom vision for my future be restored in me.

Let all spiritual strength that has been drained from my life through warfare from my past season be restored by the power of the blood of Jesus.

Let the blood of Jesus reenergize, revitalize, reactivate, revive and reset all dead potentials and spiritual gifts within me. I decree that every spiritual gift within me comes alive.

I speak to my potential and decree a supernatural explosion of all that I carry. I will not waste my potential.

By the power of the blood of Jesus, I am delivered from generational iniquities; pornography addiction; alcoholism; lust; all forms of perversion, including homosexuality, bisexuality, gender confusion, lust and masturbation; covetousness; lying; stealing; trickery; and deceit, in Jesus' name.

I decree that the blood of Jesus purges my old life. I am cleansed from every old sin issue from my former life, and I walk as a new creation in Christ.

Ezekiel ate the whole roll of the Word of God. Like Ezekiel, I consume the whole of God's Word. I open up every part of my life to be cleansed by the blood of Jesus. I keep nothing back.

The Word of God produces in me the power to rejoice in the Holy Ghost, the power to be steadfast in following God, the power to walk circumspectly, the power of holy living and the power of unashamed faithfulness in all circumstances.

I resist every assignment of religious behavior without Kingdom power that has been set against my life.

I plead the blood of Jesus over every door that I have opened to the enemy. I close every door, in Jesus' name. Every door that I opened to the enemy is forever closed, in Jesus' name.

I fall out of agreement with every work of darkness operating in me and through me, in Jesus' name.

3. PROTECTED BY THE BLOOD

The blood of Jesus is my shield against every power of darkness that would come against me.

I command every stubborn sin issue operating in my life to leave, in Jesus' name. The blood of Jesus cleanses my life. The blood of Jesus protects and shields my life.

I escape from every evil captivity attempting to operate in my life, in Jesus' name.

I command every wounded place in my soul to be healed by the power of the blood of Jesus.

I speak to the voice of trauma attempting to imprison me. I will not listen to the voice of trauma. I hear the voice of the Lord and receive my healing, in the name of Jesus.

I throw off every burden of worry, in Jesus' name.

I decree a supernatural reversal of any damage done to my life from the time I was born, in Jesus' name. The blood of Jesus overturns any such damage.

I command every spirit holding my gifts captive to let go, in Jesus' name. Because of the power of the blood of Jesus, I am fully functioning in my Kingdom identity.

Every vagabond spirit trying to operate in my life, I command you to leave. I am steadfast in the house of God, and I will not be uprooted.

I command the spirit of stagnation to leave my life, in Jesus' name. The blood of Jesus creates a flow of productivity and prosperity in my life.

I overcome by the blood of the Lamb and by the words of my testimony. I testify to the atmosphere that I am free, and whomever the Son of man sets free is really free.

I command every time waster to leave my life, in Jesus' name. The blood of Jesus is my shield to turn back every assignment against my life. I will fulfill God's plan for my life.

4. OVERCOMING ASSIGNMENTS OF DELAY

The ultimate goal of the enemy is not simply to stop your progress; he wants you to experience failure when you are at the moment of success. The enemy's purpose is to damage not only your credibility but the credibility of God as well.

The spirit of Pisgah is the spirit of "almost there." When Moses arrived at the border of the Promised Land, he went up the mountain to view it—but he was not allowed to enter. This is how delay operates. You fail at the edge of breakthrough. Business deals fall through. Growth in your ministry starts and abruptly stops. You interview for a job multiple times, and after the last interview you are told you will not get the job. You see what you want, and just as you are about to get it, something goes wrong.

As a believer, you have a finishing anointing. God is the Alpha and Omega of our lives. Jesus gives us power to finish.

I release the *shamar* anointing over my life, in Jesus' name. (*Shamar* is a Hebrew word meaning "to keep watch" and "to guard.") Everything connected to me is marked by the blood of Jesus.

By the authority and power of the blood of Jesus, I command my enemies to return what was stolen from me and to pay not less than sevenfold tribute to me.

I look to Jesus who is the author and finisher of my faith (Hebrews 12:2). The Lord will finish everything that concerns me. He will perfect everything that concerns me.

My confidence is in Jesus, the Alpha and Omega, the beginning and the end, the first and the last (Revelation 22:13).

I receive the finishing anointing in every area of my life. Jesus does not leave things half-done (we are not half-saved, half-delivered, half-restored).

I confess my sin of occasional doubt that Jesus will finish what He started in me.

I plead the blood of Jesus over every blocking spirit. Let the angels of the Lord roll away the stone blocking my financial, physical and spiritual breakthrough, in Jesus' name.

Every blocking spirit that is operating against my ministry is dismissed now, in the name of Jesus. I call every blocking spirit off of its assignment, in Jesus' name.

I will not see the goodness of the Lord without manifestation. I command every enemy blocking my blessing to be removed, in the name of Jesus.

Let God arise and all the enemies of my breakthrough be scattered, in the name of Jesus.

Let the fire of God melt away the stones hindering my blessings, in the mighty name of Jesus.

Let new wells of blessings, favor and honor spring up on my behalf, in Jesus' name.

Let every occult cloud blocking me from being seen and hindering my breakthrough be dispersed, in the name of Jesus.

Open my eyes, Lord; don't let the way before me be dark.

All secrets of the enemy that still dwell in darkness in any area of my life, let them be revealed to me now, in the name of Jesus.

Surely goodness and mercy will follow me all the days of my life.

All keys to my goodness that are still in possession of the enemy, Lord, give them to me.

All my sweat and effort of life will not be in vain, in the name of Jesus.

All evil spirits "planning" to trouble me today and every day are bound in the name of Jesus.

Lord, turn me into untouchable coals of fire that are too hot for the enemy to handle, in Jesus' name.

You said I would be the head and not the tail. I rebuke every spirit of the tail that is operating in my life.

I decree that creation cooperates with me and my destiny.

I command the land to give up my blessings now. The land will not work against me; the land works with me.

5. CUTTING OFF ATTACKS AND RELEASING BLESSINGS

Isaac answered, "I have already given Jacob the power to rule over you. And I said all his brothers would be his servants. I have given him the blessing for much grain and wine. There is nothing left to give you, my son."

But Esau continued to beg his father. "Do you have only one blessing, father? Bless me also, father!" Esau began to cry.

Then Isaac said to him, "You will not live on good land. You will not have much rain. You will have to fight to live, and you will be a slave to your brother. But when you fight to be free, you will break away from his control."

GENESIS 27:35–40 ERV

The day you get tired of satanic attacks is the day you will walk in freedom. Jacob stole his brother's birthright, and then he stole his blessings; Esau would not move forward until he was finally tired of being under his brother. The day you become tired of your current situation is the day you begin to move forward.

When Hannah cried to God, her prayer for a child was heard.

When Jabez cried to God, his prayer was heard.

The day Jacob wrestled with God's angel, he got his breakthrough.

Even the captives of the mighty shall be taken away, and the prey of the terrible be delivered; for I will contend with him who contends with you, and I will save your children. I will feed those who oppress you with their own flesh, and they shall be drunk with their own blood as with sweet wine. All flesh shall know that I, the LORD, am your Savior, and your Redeemer, the Mighty One of Jacob.

ISAIAH 49:25–26 NKJV

I rebuke all spirits of the night that come to torment me and steal my dreams.

I decree that every dark spirit cursing my dreams and attempting to stop my destiny is defeated.

Let every assignment written against me in the demonic kingdom and trying to control my life be defeated, in Jesus' name.

I rebuke all demonic agents assigned to my life.

I command total destruction of all satanic effort against my life.

Let every power of darkness hunting for my life be consumed by the fire of God.

Let any uncleanness in my life through dreams be cleansed by the blood of Jesus.

I close every door of access by the powers of darkness into my life. I welcome the presence of God, the King of the universe, into my life fresh and new today.

Let every evil incantation, hex, vex and curse, named and unnamed, that is planned and plotted against me between the hours of 12:00 and 3:00 a.m. be nullified.

Let every evil incantation, hex, vex and curse, named and unnamed, that is planned and plotted against me between the hours of 3:00 and 6:00 a.m. be nullified.

I loose myself from all bloodline bondages. I decree that I am free from every generational bondage, in Jesus' name.

I command every evil holding spirit attempting to hold me in old seasons of life to release me, in the name of Jesus.

I speak a supernatural reversal of every evil design fashioned against my life.

I decree that every hidden or open spirit of infirmity will depart from my life.

I bind every strongman operating against me, in Jesus' name. I decree that God's angelic host is warring on my behalf, defeating all of my enemies.

I command every assignment of hell operating in my life because of past mistakes to stop now, in Jesus' name. Whomever the Son sets free is free indeed, and I am free today.

I decree that every curse of backward movement is broken now. I speak success, breakthrough, increase and multiplication over my life.

Lord, make me a channel of blessing in my family, ministry, city and nation.

I take as my weapon the two-edged sword of the Spirit, and I cut down the powers of witches, wizards, familiar spirits, ancestral/familial spirits, manipulators, scanner spirits, eavesdropping spirits, evil arrows and evil decisions attempting to operate against me.

I cancel every assignment of satanic embarrassment against my life.

Let the standard of the Lord be raised against all my enemies.

Lord, use me as Your battle axe to defeat my enemies. Fight against those who fight against me.

God, let Your angels of war be released on my behalf.

I overturn every unrighteous edict written against me, and I send fire, thunder and flaming stones to destroy the powers of darkness in the air.

I bind all anti-deliverance demons in every area of my life. My entire body, mind and soul are delivered.

By the power of the prophetic decree, every satanic weapon operating against me is defeated.

By the power of the prophetic decree, I destroy the web of witchcraft, sorcery, magic and every unnamed dark power of Satan against my life. I choose to walk in victory over my enemies.

6. REBUKING DEMONIC CONFEDERACIES

I sever any satanic linkage to anyone dead or alive. Let all spiritual confederacies set against me be defeated.

I speak destruction against all protective coverings of the enemy. Let these assignments against me be consumed by the fire of God.

I cancel every careless word which I have spoken that the powers of hell are using against me. I declare crop failure over these words, in Jesus' name.

I break off any satanic attachment to any of my possessions.

I come against any and all curses issued against my future and progress.

I separate myself from all evil agreements, oaths, occult altars and shrines present in my place of birth, in Jesus' name.

Let all demonic agents stealing what belongs to me release them unto me and pay not less than sevenfold tribute to me.

I denounce all evil peace, evil agreement, evil unity, evil love, evil happiness, evil understanding, evil communication and evil gathering formed against me, in Jesus' name.

I command spirits of frustration to loose their hold over my life.

Let spirits of poverty loose their hold over my life. I break cycles of debt and poor stewardship off of my life.

Let assignments of spiritual rags loose their hold over my life. I break the cycle of grace to grass from my life. Today, I shift into the cycle and order of God's blessings, and I move from grace to grace.

I rebuke every assignment of defeat, infirmity, demotion, demonic delay, confusion, backward movement, failure to progress further and any other assignment of hell attempting to block my forward movement.

I decree that every wicked oppressor operating against me will stumble and fall.

God, I ask You to break the teeth of the ungodly gathered against me.

Let all weapons of failure fashioned against my life be consumed by the fire of God.

Let all scanner spirits and eavesdropping spirits attempting to monitor and manipulate my life be consumed by the fire of God.

I decree that every demonic confederacy that has been summoned for my sake be scattered. Let confusion come upon every demonic confederacy, and let them be routed by the power of God.

Let every demonic umbrella preventing heavenly showers from falling upon me be burned by the fire of God. Let the abundant rain of God be released in my life today and every day.

Lord, I thank You that You have given me power to pursue, overtake and recover all.

Lord, help me to crucify my flesh.

Lord, help me overcome myself.

Lord, I thank You for my season of retribution against my enemies.

I decree that every day I will receive tribute from my enemies. It is my season of supernatural payback.

I overcome by the blood of the Lamb and the words of my testimony. I declare victory today.

I testify to heaven and earth that I walk in the blessings of the head and not the tail. My life is getting better and better. My miracles are no longer delayed. Retribution against my enemies is my portion, and I receive it today.

7. DEFEATING CORDS
OF WICKEDNESS

All who compete in the games use strict training. They do this so that they can win a prize—one that doesn't last. But our prize is one that will last forever. So I run like someone who has a goal. I fight like a boxer who is hitting something, not just the air. It is my own body I fight to make it do what I want. I do this so that I won't miss getting the prize myself after telling others about it.

1 CORINTHIANS 9:25–27 ERV

Today my life will be better than yesterday. I operate in the anointing and power of better and better.

Let all demonic networks assembled and summoned for my sake be scattered and never assemble again.

I command every reinforcement of evil against me to scatter. I speak confusion over every cord of wickedness formed against me. You will not prosper over me!

I decree that every demonic vow against me spoken by me or someone else is canceled.

I speak destruction of demonic cycles and anniversary demons and all evil timetables the enemy has set against me, my family and my church. I speak a release of the Issachar anointing over my life, giving me supernatural ability to understand times and seasons and what I need to do.

I speak life over every good thing that has died in my life. I speak resurrection power over my dreams, destiny and purpose that have died, in Jesus' name.

I bind every demonic spirit working against my prayers.

I choose to abide in the secret place of God (Psalm 91:1); therefore my life is hidden in God. According to Colossians 3:2–4, I set my mind on things above, not on things on the earth. I died, and my life is hidden with Christ in God. When Christ who is my life appears, I also will appear with Him in glory.

I revoke all conscious and unconscious covenants with the spirit of death. I will live out the number of my days in the earth.

Lord, I submit my tongue to You; take control.

I repent on behalf of both sides of my bloodline for any covenant-breaking spirits and innocent bloodshed, including abortions.

I repent on behalf of both sides of my bloodline for not honoring the principles of rest, work and worship.

I refuse to wage war against myself; therefore I set a watch over my mouth. I will not be careless with my words.

Lord, wake me from any form of spiritual sleep.

Let every evil seed planted by fear into my life be uprooted, in Jesus' name.

Lord, let my life be a demonstration of the power of Your Kingdom.

I command all physical and spiritual sickness to flee from my life by the power of the blood of Jesus.

Let the enemy fall into the pit dug for me.

Let my life experience divine favor in every area.

I release the woe of God against any vessel sent by the enemy to do me harm.

Let the tongues of my enemies be divided and confused, and let the counsels of the wicked be broken.

Lord, give me miracles that will dumbfound the world.

I command my enemies to become a footstool, and I trample the powers of darkness under my feet.

Lord, let me experience victory in every area of my life.

Any good thing that the enemy has removed from my life, let it be returned today with retribution.

I call forth any blessings that have been locked up. Locked-up blessings, come out of captivity today and return to my life.

8. OVERCOMING MARINE SPIRITS

Marine spirits are spirits and principalities associated with water and the sea.[1] Leviathan, for example, is a large sea serpent (see Isaiah 27:1), and similar spirits are described in Ezekiel 29:3–4, Job 41, and Revelation 17:1–2. Some are referred to as Poseidon, Neptune, Sea Hag and Sea Dragon. Proud and arrogant, they are ruling spirits that assert their control in coastal cities. A whole kingdom of darkness operates from under the waters and under the seas.

"I am against you, Pharaoh, king of Egypt. You are the great monster lying beside the Nile River. You say, 'This is my river! I made this river!' But I will put hooks in your jaws. The fish in the Nile River will stick to your scales. I will pull you and your fish up out of your rivers and onto the dry land. You will fall on the ground, and no one will pick you up or bury you. I will give you to the wild animals and birds. You will be their food"... God said, "Why will I do these things? Because you said, 'This is my river. I made this river.' So I am against you. I am against the many branches of your Nile River.

EZEKIEL 29:3–5, 9–10 ERV

---

1. John Eckhardt, *Title of the Apostolic Dictionary* (Chicago, IL John Eckhardt, 2002, s.v. "marine spirits."

Greater is He who is in me than any power on earth and in the waters. I am born of God, and I have overcome the world with my faith.

In faith I come against evil strongholds of any marine kingdom. In faith I declare your waters are polluted. I speak the blood of Jesus over every body of water.

I overturn every ruling spirit enthroned against me. By faith I trample upon serpents and scorpions. I spoil demonic palaces, bind their operations and set the captives free.

There will be no reinforcement or evil reunion of this power against me, and I seal every confession with the blood of Jesus.

Any witchcraft practiced under any water against my life, receive immediate judgment by the fire of God.

Let every evil altar under any water, upon which certain evils are done against me, be burned by the fire of God.

Let the judgment of God be released against every priest ministering at any evil altar against my life, family or ministry.

I decree that any power under the water remotely controlling my life is defeated and I am free.

Every marine demon working against my health, my family, my relationships, my church or my city, I command you to receive God's judgment of fire.

I pull down every stronghold of bewitchment, enchantment, jinx or divination fashioned against my life, my family, my marriage or my church by marine demons.

Any marine witchcraft chain keeping my hands and feet from prospering is broken, in Jesus' name.

Any evil ever done against me through marine demons' witchcraft, oppression and manipulation be reversed by the blood of Jesus.

I bind up and off my life every assignment of the sea hag, sea dragon, sea serpent and any other dark power operating against me.

Every power of hell operating against me above, on or beneath the water is broken now, in Jesus' name.

I decree that the waters of trouble will not overflow in my life today or any other day.

9. PRAYERS FOR TERRITORIES AND NATIONS

Lord, I ask that You release what I need so that my need can be supplied. Lord, open the door of business to me.

Lord, I ask that You send the manifestation of the Holy Spirit to remind the Church in every nation of the Great Commission—to disciple their nations so that they will come back to Jehovah. [Pray for your nation by name.]

Let the unity of the Spirit return to the Church in America; there is neither Jew nor Greek, bound nor free, male nor female in Christ. We are all one. Let unity prevail.

You have established America as a model to the nations. Let America return to Your original intent for her.

Awaken the Church in every nation from slumber. Awaken us, Lord, from a place of slumber. Show us where we have slipped and fallen away or slept and the enemy has come to sow tares in our fields.

Lord, send angels to patrol my territory as the night progresses. I decree that tares will not be sown in my fields tonight. I draw the bloodline of Jesus over my life and my inheritance.

Let new networks of prayer be raised up that intercede for communities and nations according to Your will. I decree that these times of intercession will not be religious or legalistic. I decree that these will be times when the fire of the Lord is released from our lips to consume our enemies.

Lord, give me favor in every endeavor of my life. Give me favor to share the Gospel, and make me an example of righteousness so that others can be drawn to the Lord through my life.

Let favor surround me like a shield all the time. Let favor surround my city. I decree that the rate of violence is decreasing in my city.

I plead the blood of Jesus over the school system in my area. Let minority students in my city begin to excel exponentially. I decree exposure of teachers who berate and mistreat students. Let them be terminated from their positions.

Let every pedophile, child molester, drug abuser and physical abuser of children working or volunteering in the school system be exposed and terminated. Let them be charged with the appropriate crime and incarcerated. Then let someone representing Your Kingdom share the Gospel with them. Let their hearts be turned to You in prison so that they can extend the Kingdom of God over Islam during their incarceration.

Cause the enemies of the Church in America to begin to promote God's prophetic purposes for the Church. Let the wineskin of religion that has veiled the Church and distorted Your voice be broken, and let the paradigm of the Church shift to reflect Your forward-moving Kingdom.

I pray for the media landscape of my nation. I decree that Kingdom believers will overtake Hollywood. I decree that new social media outlets that reflect the Kingdom of God are being invented. They will supersede current social media platforms in growth! I decree an overturning of laws allowing child pornography. I decree that new television stations that reflect the Kingdom of God are being created. I decree new print media outlets that supersede existing outlets. The assignment of propaganda is broken today—let there be truth in media.

I decree a drying up of publishing houses for pornography. Let a holy outcry from the Church be released against pornography on television, in print media and in other forms of media.

I decree that the airwaves belong to God.

Lord, raise up individuals who will redeem media and change it from a vessel for spreading more harm than good to an instrument of educating and discipling society for the Kingdom.

Lord, I ask that You raise up creative entertainment that will build rather than destroy the fabric of my nation.

[If you have been bound by pornography, pray this prayer daily.] I repent for participating in and supporting unclean media expressions like pornography, X- and R-rated movies, etc. I will not put anything unclean before me eyes. I will not meditate upon the wickedness depicted in pornographic or sexually explicit material. I am set free today and every day!

10. RELEASING PERSONAL DESTINY

I renounce every assignment of inherited poverty in my life, in the name of Jesus.

I refuse to reap a harvest of evil, in Jesus' name. I decree that good things are being released to me each day.

I decree that the divine favor of God covers my life, in Jesus' name.

Lord, make my life a terror and dread to the enemy.

Strengthen my hands to break every stronghold of the enemy in every area of my life, family and ministry, in the name of Jesus.

Let my enemies suffer public disgrace, in Jesus' name. Let the table of the Lord be prepared for me to eat in the presence of my enemies.

Lord release Your fire and destroy every evil imagination against any area of my life, in Jesus' name.

Lord, expose and disgrace all the schemes of Satan ever devised against me through any source and at any time.

I forsake every personal sin that has given ground to the enemy, in the name of Jesus. Deliver me from secret sin.

I reclaim the ground that I have lost to the enemy. This is my season of retribution!

I command every power of the enemy working against my progress to take leave now, in the name of Jesus. I break every assignment of failure attempting to operate against me.

I sever myself from Satan and any strange power, in the name of Jesus.

I remove the right of any strange power fashioned against me by the power of the blood of Jesus, my Redeemer.

I break every bondage of inherited sickness, in the name of Jesus. Inherited sickness will no longer plague me.

I declare that premature death and sickness have no power over me. I will live out the number of days assigned to me, and I shall fulfill my purpose in the earth.

I break every bondage of inherited mental illness, in the name of Jesus. I have a sound mind.

I command every spirit of infirmity to leave my life now, in Jesus' name. My next doctor's appointment will reflect healing.

I decree that my children will walk in their God-ordained destiny.

I decree that my children walk in divine health. I cancel every assignment against their focus and attention. I cancel every assignment of diabetes and blood disorders. I cancel every assignment of cognitive delay. I cancel every assignment of nightmares and night terrors.

Every spirit of the Antichrist assigned to my children, I call you off of your assignment now, in Jesus' name.

I call every assignment of rebellion against authority operating in my children off of your assignment, in Jesus' name.

My children are protected against assignments of rape, molestation and kidnap.

My children will not be the victim of accidental death including, drowning, or murder.

My children will not be the victim of spirits of suicide and self-destruction including self-mutilation.

My children will not be victims of bullying, violence and ostracism. My children walk in favor with God and man.

I call my prodigal children back to the house of God. Every prodigal in my family, I call you back to the house of God. I remove every hedge of thorns around the lives of prodigals that stands between them and returning to the house of God.

I break every bondage of isolation that prevents me from connecting to other believers, in the name of Jesus.

I receive healing from soul wounds, in the name of Jesus.

Let every spirit of wasting attempting to operate against my health, family and finances be broken off of my life, in the name of Jesus.

I stand against every addictive desire in my life, in Jesus' name.

I release creative miracles in every area of my life.

I command the spirit of destruction operating against me, my family, my church and my city to leave now. I call you off of your assignment, in Jesus' name.

Lord, take me from where I am to where You want me to be, in Jesus' name.

Lord, establish me in truth, godliness and faithfulness.

Lord, add favor to my work.

Lord, add increase in my work.

Lord, add profitability to my work.

Lord, promote and preserve my life.

I will not forfeit my destiny. You created me with a purpose in mind, and I decree that I will fulfill my destiny.

Lord, I repent for neglecting Your purpose for my life. Today I choose to embrace who You have called me to be and what You have called me to do.

I am a chosen vessel in the hand of the Lord. God has raised me up for such a time as this. I will not be unprofitable in the earth. Today and every day, I live the destiny God has assigned me.

I confess Jeremiah 29:11 over my life today. God has given me a good future and a hope. God is bringing me to a place of success in life and ministry!

11. DEFEATING BEELZEBUB

The name Beelzebub *(or* Baalzebub*) means "Lord of the flies" or "Lord of dung." Unclean spirits traffic in unsubmitted areas of our lives. These unclean spirits work to entrench themselves in such areas in an attempt to establish a stronghold. A stronghold is often established in a way that can prevent your gift from operating.*

Strongholds can be broken, however. Flies do not live forever; their lives last only about 28 days. Whatever is operating against you will break in 40 days if you commit to spending time with the Lord, for the number 40 represents separation. Moses was on the mountain with God for 40 days, as was Jesus in the wilderness.

I rebuke every spirit of the fly attempting to operate in my life. I will not feed on anything dead or dry. Today I choose life.

Today I choose to separate myself from every unclean thing. I am called and chosen by God, and I refuse to be defiled.

I plead the blood of Jesus over a spirit of careless prayerlessness, in the name of Jesus. As I pray, I am being rooted and grounded in the eternal things of God.

I decree that I will not only be a worshiper in corporate gatherings; beginning today, I will become a secret worshiper. Every assignment of hell that has come after my worship is defeated today. There is no disagreement between my private life of worship and my public life.

Every assignment of spiritual dryness, dullness of hearing and hardness of heart is broken from my life today.

I am free, and whomever the Son of man sets free is really free!

I plead the blood of Jesus over every assignment that comes against my mind, preventing me from being focused on eternity, in the name of Jesus.

Today I remind the enemy of the power of the blood of Jesus and command every assignment set against me to fail.

I decree Psalm 72:4. God is judging my oppressors today. Today He is breaking my oppressors in pieces.

According to Psalm 72:9, I decree that my enemies will bow and lick the dust, in Jesus' name!

I decree the authority of the blood of Jesus over every evil assignment holding up my provision, in Jesus' name.

I decree the authority of the blood of Jesus over every assignment that keeps me from progressing in life and ministry. Today I begin to progress in a new way. There is a new momentum being released over me right now. I am becoming unstoppable by the power of Holy Spirit.

Let the joy of the Lord strengthen me. I decree His right hand of righteousness upholds me. The countenance of the Lord brightens my life. The power of depression and sadness is broken off of me. I command the spirit of misery to leave my life now.

Today the horn of His salvation is pouring out anointing on me. I plead the blood of Jesus against every evil spirit keeping me in a low place. Today, I am rising in a new way. My life is soaked with anointing today.

I will not fall into the pit of my enemies today. Every pit that has been dug for me the enemy will fall into.

Through the blood of Jesus, I have life. No sickness can dwell in me.

Thank You, Father, for the provision of the blood of Jesus.

I command every work of darkness in my life to dry up to the roots by the power of the blood of Jesus.

I plead the blood of Jesus against every assignment of failure at the edge of a miracle. Every assignment at the point of my breakthrough is cast down now, in Jesus' name.

Every demonic assignment that comes to frustrate and hinder my destiny is cast down now.

I decree that I walk in the light and blood of Jesus, and I have been redeemed out of the hand of the enemy.

Through the blood of Jesus, I am justified, sanctified and made holy with God's holiness.

Let the power of the cross and blood of Jesus stand between me and every demonic power that would try to operate against me.

Let every wound in my soul be healed, in the name of Jesus.

Every assignment set against my destiny and my purpose is canceled today.

I set my day and night in Kingdom order. Creation cooperates with me and not against me.

Blessings come to me and not curses. Life comes to me and not death.

My faith is activated in a new way. I have been cleansed by the blood of Jesus.

12. RELEASING THE VOICE OF THE LORD

Lord, I thank You that Your voice thunders from heaven, all the enemies will be scattered, and it will be clear that it is time for all people to praise the Lord.

I decree that the voice of the Lord will thunder above every other voice that might try to arise in every season.

God, I thank You that my help and defense come from *You* and not from any demon. You alone are the Lord of every day!

Lord, I ask that Your voice be released like thunder to drown out and silence the uproar of every satanic or evil voice being proclaimed in my life, family, community and nation.

I declare that Your voice will drown out and silence the voice of murder, mayhem, destruction and premature death. Every spirit of Abaddon and Apollyon is silenced throughout every city with high minority populations.

Let the voice of the Lord be released against assignments of genocide and ethnic cleansing, in Jesus' name.

Lord, let Your voice be released against abortion in my nation.

I decree that the voice of the Lord will be released against all forms of sex trafficking, including child sex trafficking.

I pray that the voice of sanity and reason will prevail over every voice of confusion, chaos and anarchy in every gate of society in my nation (see Acts 19:37–40).

I decree that men and women will begin to find their identities and refuse drugs, murder and perversion.

Lord, I ask that You arise and rebuke the forces of the satanic heavenly host. Let the power and might of every satanic force be shaken today and every day.

Lord, let Your voice be released against every demonic foundation.

According to Haggai 2:6–9, let every demonic foundation be shaken out of its place. Lord, let Your voice be released to shake the nations. Let the wealth of nations flow into the Church so that Your Kingdom can be advanced in the earth.

I pray that every cloud that has covered the people of God will be blown away by Your breath.

Lord, I ask that You help every believer know what things to uproot, tear down, destroy and overthrow, and also what to plant and build. I pray that You will give me grace and strength to do what You have purposed for my life.

I possess the gates of the enemy today and every day!

13. Overcoming Weakness

> *The power to overcoming is in the blood of Jesus and the indwelling of Holy Spirit. We must develop consistent times for prayer if we are to experience all that Jesus paid for.*

We are completely free to enter the Most Holy Place. We can do this without fear because of the blood sacrifice of Jesus. We enter through a new way that Jesus opened for us.

HEBREWS 10:19 ERV

I receive the virtues, strength, power, might and anointing in the blood of Jesus.

Let the blood quicken everything that is dead within me. Let Kingdom vision be restored in me.

Let all spiritual strength that has been drained from my life be restored by the power of the blood of Jesus.

I rebuke every assignment of spiritual wasting attempting to operate in my life.

Let the blood of Jesus reenergize, revitalize, reactivate, revive and reset all dead potentials and spiritual gifts within me. Those things that died within me in the last season, that were ordained to live, are being resurrected today.

Let the blood of Jesus cleanse me from all inherited or self-acquired iniquities, including generational iniquities, pornography addiction, alcoholism, all forms of perversion, sex addictions, lust, masturbation, covetousness, lying, stealing, trickery and deceit, in Jesus' name.

I rebuke and resist every generational assignment of iniquity trying to capture my life. I will not be ensnared and enslaved by issues that captured my forefathers.

I declare Joel 3:10 over my life. Today I am strong. My spiritual strength increases every day.

I rebuke and resist spiritual weakness. I am strong in the power of His might as I stand against darkness, in Jesus' name.

You said I would be the head and not the tail. I rebuke every spirit of the tail that is operating in my life.

I command the land to give up my blessings now. The land will not work against me, the land works with me.

Let my point of ridicule be converted to a miracle.

Let unusual doors of blessing and favor open in my life today that will change the rest of my life.

Let every stubborn strongman assigned against me fall to the ground and become powerless to hinder me.

Let every spirit of Balaam hired to curse me fall.

Let the stronghold of every spirit of Korah, Dathan and Abiram mobilizing against me be smashed to pieces.

Let every spirit of Sanballat and Tobiah planning evil against me be defeated, in Jesus' name.

Let every spirit of Goliath attempting to operate against me, my family or nation, be defeated.

Let every spirit of character assassination be defeated, in Jesus' name.

Let all satanic manipulations aimed at changing my destiny be cast down.

Let every scanner spirit, evil eye and third eye of the medium be frustrated. Let them fail to locate me as I dwell in the secret place of the Most High God.

I command that the evil assignment intended to hinder my advancement, so that I go backward instead of forward, be broken.

Let all evil advice given against my favor be exposed for what it is.

I cancel any enchantments, curses, hexes, vexes, spells and incantations against me.

Let all iron-like curses break into pieces, in Jesus' name.

I resist every assignment of spiritual failure. Every cycle of weakness operating in my life is broken today and every day.

14. PRAYERS FOR REVELATION

Lord, in Psalm 32:8 (ERV) You said, "I will teach you and guide you in the way you should live. I will watch over you and be your guide." Watch over me and guide me today and every day.

According to Proverbs 3:5, I trust the Lord completely, and I do not depend on my own knowledge.

God, make me completely sure of what You want by giving me all the wisdom and spiritual understanding I need (Colossians 1:9).

"He reveals deep and secret things; He knows what is in the darkness, and light dwells with Him" (Daniel 2:22 NKJV). Lord, release great revelation unto me today.

According to Ephesians 1:17, I decree that the God of our Lord Jesus Christ, the Father of glory, is giving me the spirit of wisdom and revelation in the knowledge of Him.

"The secret of the LORD is with them that fear him; and he will shew them his covenant" (Psalm 25:14 KJV). Lord, may the covenant benefits and blessings be released to me today and every day.

"The secret things belong to the LORD our God, but those things which are revealed belong to us and to our children forever, that we may do all the words of this law" (Deuteronomy 29:29 NKJV). Lord, reveal secrets from Your heart unto me today.

I decree Jeremiah 33:3 (NKJV) over my life today. As I call to the Lord, You will show me great and mighty things that I did not know. I will receive downloads of revelation as I call to You.

Lord, I thank You for the revelation power of the Holy Spirit.

Lord, open up my spiritual understanding and teach me deep and secret things.

Lord, guide and direct me in knowing Your mind for my family, ministry, city and nation.

I stand against all satanic attachments that may seek to confuse my decisions.

I bind the activities of lust, ungodly infatuation, ungodly family pressure, demonic manipulation in dreams and visions, attachment to the wrong choice, confusing revelations, spiritual blindness and deafness, unprofitable advice and ungodly impatience.

Lord, make Your plan plain before my face.

Lord, You are the revealer of secrets. Make known unto me Your choice for me in every area of my life.

Holy Spirit, open my eyes and help me to make the right choices every day.

Lord, I thank You for the testimonies that will follow these prayers.

15. DOMINION AND VICTORY

I decree that this is the day of blessings, fruitfulness, multiplication, replenishing (abundance, filling, consecration, arming, satisfying), subduing and conquest.

I take authority over every assignment of disappointment that is trying to overtake me.

I bind up and off of my life every spirit of hope deferred, lack of expectation and discouragement, in Jesus' name.

I pray that any portion that should be yielded to me from creation will be released today and every day.

I decree that creation will cooperate with God's will for my life, family, ministry and city. I decree that I flourish. My life is getting better and better. My quality of life will reflect the blessings and favor of the Lord.

I decree that any assignment from hell that has been operating against God's purpose in and for my life, community, family and church is being arrested by the angel of the Lord.

I pray that God's original blueprint for man be fully restored.

I pray for the restoration of dominion over creation as God intended. I decree that I will walk in dominion in every area of life as God intended.

I decree that Jesus will rise and shine in my life, heart, ministry, family, city, region and nation as the bright and morning star (Revelation 22:16). Lord, I ask You to arise in greater measure and degree. I open my heart and say, "Arise, O Lord, in me!"

I cancel every assignment of the dragon, sea serpent and sea hag including all the words (waters) they have poured from their mouths to flood me and my family, city, community and nation.

I pray that the earth will open its mouth and swallow up all of the waters the dragon has spewed out to flood me. Creation will not operate against me.

> *Then the dragon poured water out of its mouth like a river. It poured the water toward the woman so that the flood would carry her away. But the earth helped the woman. The earth opened its mouth and swallowed the river that came from the mouth of the dragon.*
>
> **REVELATION 12:15–16 ERV**

I decree that the stars in heaven will reflect the bright and morning star, Jesus! Creation will not operate against me. Creation will speak forth the praises of God, and there is no speech or language in which its voice will not be heard.

I pray that every human kingdom messenger, called to advance the mandate of God in the earth will reflect the glory of the Lord and walk righteously, justly and in purity.

Lord, I thank You that You created mankind to walk in dominion over every created thing.

Lord, I thank You that this is not only the day You have made, it is the day of multiplication, replenishing abundance and subduing all things under Your rule. Holy Spirit, I ask You to teach me and my family how to make these values a reality in our day-to-day, walking-around life.

Lord, I thank You that You are love. There is no other love that can be as complete as the love of God. I pray that Your love will be made manifest more and more in relationships in my territory, starting with me.

Lord, I thank You that Your love is redemptive. Your love for me caused You to secure salvation for the world through the shed blood of Jesus.

I decree that the earth will manifest everything I need to be successful in my God-ordained destiny.

Let the dayspring arise in the hearts of all true men and women of God to bring hope and comfort to families, cities and communities.

I decree that every false son of the dawn—those who project themselves as the nation's light but are of the devil—will be laid low and cast down. Let false brethren in the Church be exposed.

Everything that needs to be birthed today will be birthed so that the plan of God for my life will be on course—for me individually and for my nation—and will be birthed at its proper time.

Lord, I ask You to rescue Kingdom citizens and their families from all who hate them. I rebuke every anti-Christ spirit.

Lord, I pray that representatives in every gate of society, those who are kings and priests before You, will arise and take their places. I pray for revelation for those who do not recognize their role as Kingdom representatives in our families, cities and nations.

God, I repent for misusing my position and exposing people to a counterfeit spirit. I pray that the spirit of godly repentance will fall on every Kingdom messenger who is misusing his or her position of authority and exposing people to a counterfeit spirit.

Lord, deliver Your Church. Bring Your Church back to her identity as a house of prayer for all nations. Bring Your Church back to the place of passionately pursuing You above everything else. Deliver Your Church from religion and pseudo–Kingdom behavior. Let the Church draw near to You with clean hands and a pure heart.

16. INCREASING PRODUCTIVITY

I silence the voices of all of my oppressors, critics and naysayers.

I decree judgment over every assignment of wickedness operating against my life, ministry, family and finances.

I decree that this is my season of manifestation of God's promises to me.

I decree that goodness and mercy follow me. God has determined that He would satisfy me with good things. Let good things manifest all around me.

I speak life over every project I have started. I decree that every project I have started will live out its divinely ordained life span (see Ecclesiastes 3:1) and will not die prematurely.

I decree that I am redeeming time. I will not waste time, and my productivity in God's purposes for my life will continually increase.

Let every time waster operating in my life be exposed, in Jesus' name.

Let every toxic relationship in my life be exposed. Lord, send me relationships that will encourage and support me.

Lord, I ask You for new beginnings. I ask that You bless every endeavor that I have started according to Your purpose. Let the foundation of my day reflect Your Kingdom. Let there be a display of righteousness, justice and equity in my life.

Lord, help me to keep watch over my mouth so that I will speak only that which will cause Your Kingdom to come in every situation.

Give me words that will edify and build up Your purpose in my life. Do this for all believers.

Put Your words in my mouth so that I will plant the heavens and lay the foundations of the earth for each day. Lord, give me the words to shape this day according to Your purposes.

I refuse to speak words that will release assignments of devils against me.

Lord, I ask for redemption of time. I repent of any area where I have wasted time or misused time in the past days.

Lord, help us to understand the value of using time properly, including keeping time and using it for Your purposes above everything else.

Lord, help me to schedule my activities according to Your timetable. Holy Spirit, help me to be obedient to adjusting my time according to Your purposes.

Let the Issachar anointing be released in my life today and everyday so that I will understand times and seasons and what I need to do according to 1 Chron. 12:32 (NKJV).

Lord, let me be filled with the nature of the Lamb in Revelation 5 to do what has been impossible in the past, especially in the area of Your will for my life.

Give me humility like the Lamb. Give me a gentle spirit so that I will obey You.

Give me insight and revelation as I enter the night. Protect my mind and soul as I rest.

Give me Kingdom dreams and visions as I rest tonight and every night. I arrest the growth of every evil seed that the enemy tries to plant in my life as I sleep tonight.

Give me creative dreams as I sleep. Give me creative downloads throughout the day.

I take control of the gate of the night. The enemy will not take control of any part of the night in my life, family and city, whether I am awake or asleep. I will awaken refreshed, filled with creativity and productivity. I was created to possess the gates of the enemy.

I command the night to reveal the knowledge of the glory of God. I reject all forms of knowledge that come from the occult, witchcraft, soothsaying or demonic trances.

17. RELEASING JUDGMENT AND VINDICATION OF THE LORD

I release judgment on the wicked who plan devious events during the hours of darkness.

Lord, preserve the fruits of my life. I speak fruitfulness over my life and endeavors.

I decree preservation of my territory and God's purposes in my territory.

I cry out to the Lord for the lives of our children and families. I pray for our neighborhoods and communities.

Lord, preserve the families in our churches. Let marriages be strong. Push families into their destinies. Lord, visit the foundation of every family.

Lord, do a new thing among men and women. I pray that they will find their identity in God and not in the temporary fashions of the world. Let oppressed men and women experience vindication and freedom as they take their places in Your Kingdom.

Lord, push my family into its destiny. Reveal every redemptive purpose for my family. Show me exactly why You created us as You did, why You set our habitation and boundaries the way You did. Lord, show us why You equipped us in certain ways and how we can harness that equipping to fulfill Your purposes.

Lord, I send the judgment of the Lord upon every spirit of wickedness in the land. I decree the Word of God will be established in the land, resulting in freedom from injustice and every oppression. I decree punishment for the wicked in the high places. I decree that idols and evil forces in the land receive their portion of judgment from the Lord.

Lord, You are the Righteous Judge. Let every man and woman unjustly incarcerated be vindicated.

NOTES

_____

_____

_____

_____

_____

_____

_____

_____

_____

_____

_____

_____

_____

_____

_____

_____

_____

_____

_____

_____

Part II
Advanced
Engagement

18. UNDERSTANDING THE PRAYER WATCHES

At Creation, God established the order of time in day and night that governs the daily pattern of our lives. While we should always pray, there are times during the day and night when a specific anointing emerges to accomplish God's Kingdom purposes. It was during the last watch of the night, for example, that God delivered the Israelites from Egypt: "And it came to pass that in the morning watch the LORD looked unto the host of the Egyptians through the pillar of fire and of the cloud, and troubled the host of the Egyptians" (Exodus 14:24). By watching in prayer through the four watches of the day and the four watches of the night, we also can take part in the Lord's Kingdom purposes.

We find several words in Scripture that describe the watches; one of them is the Hebrew word *ashmu-rah*[2], meaning a "watch" or "period of time." It is used for the night watch, such as in Psalm 119:148 (NKJV): "My eyes are awake through the night watches, that I may meditate on Your word." Jesus Himself did this in Matthew 14:23, when He prayed through the night alone before returning to His disciples in an astonishing way: "And in the fourth watch of the night, Jesus went unto them, walking on the sea" (verse 25). May the understanding of the watches be released upon you as you endeavor to become a proficient practitioner of prayer and see more of your prayers answered.

---

2. Strong's Exhaustive Concordance

Division of the Night Watches[3]

First watch of the night: 6:00 p.m. to 9:00 p.m.
Second watch of the night: 9:00 p.m. to 12:00 midnight
Third watch of the night: 12:00 midnight to 3:00 a.m.
Fourth watch of the night: 3:00 a.m. to 6:00 a.m.

Division of the Day Watches

First watch of the day: 6:00 a.m. to 9:00 a.m.
Second watch of the day: 9:00 a.m. to 12:00 noon
Third watch of the day: 12:00 noon to 3:00 p.m.
Fourth watch of the day: 3:00 p.m. to 6:00 p.m.

---

3. Bako, Abu, Praying Through The Gates of Time, 1977, 1978, 1984

19. First Watch of the Night

6:00 P.M. TO 9:00 P.M.

G od's cycle of time runs from evening to morning: "And the evening and the morning were the first day" (Genesis 1:5). The evening is the link between day and night, and this first watch can be seen as a transition watch between the two.

Distinctions of This Watch: A Time for New Beginnings

- It was during this watch that Jesus broke bread with His disciples to commemorate His death. The first watch is a time to renew our covenant with God (communion) and to appropriate the provision in the blood covenant.

- This watch carries an anointing of deliverance. The Lion of the tribe of Judah was able to break every yoke, including the seals on the scroll in the hand of God, thus opening the title deed of the universe (see Revelation 5:1–4). That Lion, however, appeared as a Lamb. Humility is a source of strength for the Lamb of God, which is why during this watch He put a towel around His waist and washed the feet of the disciples.

- Witchcraft activity is high during this watch (see Psalm 59:1–7; Ezekiel 13:20–21). Witches often engage in the practice of astral projection, during which they touch realms of darkness. This is described as the astral body leaving the physical body and traveling into astral realms—much like "flying." Another way to understand this practice is the souls of witches connecting to the second heaven for power and information. The first watch is the most active time for witches to engage in this way because they intend to take hold of the gates of the day. This is the period to pray and silence all the voices of the oppressors and to release judgment on the wicked.

- Pray for every project you have started. Decree that every project you started will live out its divinely ordained life span (see Ecclesiastes 3:1) and will not die prematurely.

- This is a time to redeem time. Ask the Lord to show you how to redeem lost times and seasons in your life and ministry. Pray prophetically to determine who enters and consumes your time. Pray against time wasters.

- The foundation of society is families. The foundation of a healthy church is families. When families are aligned with God and follow after righteous patterns, it is reflected in society. This is a time to pray for families.

PRAYERS, DECREES AND CONFESSIONS

Lord, I ask You for beginnings. I ask that You bless every endeavor that I have started according to Your purpose. Let the foundation of my day reflect Your Kingdom. Let there be a display of righteousness, justice and equity in my life.

Lord, help me to keep a watch over my mouth so that I will speak only that which will cause Your Kingdom to come in every situation.

Give me words that will edify and build up Your purpose throughout creation. Do this for all believers.

Put Your words in my mouth so that I will plant the heavens and lay the foundations of the earth for today. Lord, give me the words to shape this day according to Your purposes.

Lord, I ask for redemption of time. I repent of any area in which I have wasted time or misused time in the past days.

Lord, help me to understand the value of using time properly, including keeping time and using it for Your covenant purposes above everything else.

Lord help me to schedule my activities according to Your timetable. Holy Spirit, help me to be obedient to adjusting my time according to Your covenant purposes for my life.

Lord, let me be filled with the nature of the Lamb in Revelation 5 to do what has been impossible in the past, especially in the area of Your will for my life.

Give me humility like the Lamb. Give me a gentle spirit so that I will obey You.

Give me insight and revelation as I enter the night. Protect my mind and soul as I rest.

Give me Kingdom dreams and visions as I rest tonight. I arrest every evil seed that the enemy will try to plant in my life as I sleep tonight.

I take control of the gate of the night. The enemy will not take control of any part of the night in my life, family and city, whether I am awake or asleep. I am delivered from every assignment of the enemy during this time.

Let angels with flaming sword guard the gates of every watch on my behalf.

I command the earth to reject any command from the kingdom of darkness during the night against me, my family and my church.

I silence the voices of witches who want to take hold of the gates of the day (Psalm 59:1–7; Ezekiel 13:20–21). I command that every assignment of witches that cause the souls of men to fly be broken.

I call every spirit of mind control manifesting itself in delusions off of its assignment. My thoughts are clear, and I do not hallucinate. I command every assignment of mind control and mental confusion to let go, in Jesus' name.

Lord, let Your voice be released, and silence every other voice speaking from the kingdom of darkness trying to control the day.

I command the night to reveal the knowledge of the glory of God and reject every other knowledge being exposed to it. The night will not operate against me, my family or ministry.

Let judgment be released on the wicked who plan any devious events during the hours of darkness.

Lord, preserve the fruits of my life. I speak fruitfulness over my life and endeavors.

I decree preservation of my territory and God's purposes in my territory. I have been anointed to walk in dominion in the earth. Let the gates of my city open to welcome the King of glory.

I decree that entire families will come to You, God, through evangelism efforts of Kingdom people.

I cry out to the Lord for the lives of children and families. I pray for the neighborhoods and communities in my city. I rebuke spirits of violence, murder and mayhem that would try to operate during this time; I decree your power is broken, in Jesus' name.

I ask the Lord to preserve the families in the churches of my city. Let marriages be strong. Push families into their destinies. Lord, visit the foundation of every family. Let broken families be healed and restored, in Jesus' name.

PART II I pray for men in my community. Lord, I ask that You begin a new thing among men. I pray that men will find their identity in God and not in the temporary fashions of the world.

I pray that men will return to Your original purposes as leaders and protectors. Give them dreams and visions about the great destiny You have planned for them.

Lord, push my family into our destiny. Reveal every redemptive purpose for my family. Show us exactly why You created us as You did, why You set our habitation and boundaries the way You did. Lord, show us why You equipped us in certain ways and how we can harness that equipping to fulfill Your purposes.

I send the judgment of the Lord upon every spirit of wickedness in the land. I decree the Word of God will be established in the land, resulting in freedom from injustice and every oppression. I decree punishment for the wicked in high places of the land. I decree that idols and evil forces in the land receive their portion from the Lord.

20. SECOND WATCH OF THE NIGHT

9:00 P.M. TO 12:00 MIDNIGHT

The second watch of the night is a time to pray for favor and provision. Exodus 3:21–22 and chapters 11–12 show how God made the Egyptians favorable to Israel; as a result, Israel did not leave Egypt empty handed, for the Egyptians gave Israel whatever they asked for. "And I will give this people favor in the sight of the Egyptians. And it shall come to pass that, when ye go, ye shall not go empty" (Exodus 3:21). The apostle Paul also received favor from his captors during this watch:

> The young man said, "Some Jews have decided to ask you to bring Paul down to their council meeting tomorrow. They want you to think that they plan to ask Paul more questions. But don't believe them! More than 40 of them are hiding and waiting to kill him. They have all promised not to eat or drink until they have killed him. Now they are waiting for you to say yes."
>
> The commander sent the young man away, telling him, "Don't tell anyone that you have told me about their plan." Then the commander called two army officers. He said to them, "I need some men to go to Caesarea. Get 200 soldiers ready. Also, get 70 soldiers on horses and 200 men to carry spears. Be ready to leave at nine o'clock tonight. Get some horses for Paul to ride so that he can be taken to Governor Felix safely."
>
> **ACTS 23:20–24 ERV**

Pray for protection and strength to overcome.

DISTINCTIONS OF THIS WATCH:
DIVINE FAVOR AND PROTECTION

- The second watch of the night was the watch Jesus kept preceding His arrest (Matthew 26:36–46). Jesus asked His disciples to watch with Him as He prayed in the Garden, but the disciples slept during this critical time. As you pray during this watch, ask the Lord to release an outpouring of the Spirit of grace, prayer and supplication (Zechariah 12:10). Ask Him to help you be awake, watching in prayer.

- Ask also for a sense of urgency to accomplish His will, just as Israel ate the first Passover with their coats on so that they could leave Egypt quickly during the second watch.

PRAYERS, DECREES AND CONFESSIONS

Lord, I ask that You send the manifestation of the Holy Spirit to remind the Church in every nation of the Great Commission—to disciple their nations so that they will come back to Jehovah.

I pray that the belief system of the nations would align with Your Word, beginning with my nation.

Let the unity of the Spirit return to the Church in America; there is neither Jew nor Greek, bound nor free, male nor female in Christ. We are all one. Let unity prevail.

You have established America as a model to the nations. Let America return to Your original intent for her.

Let the nations be delivered from spirits of humanism and intellectualism that prevent them from coming to the Lord.

Let every false belief system be exposed in our nations, in Jesus' name.

I decree the overturning of false systems of worship and occult worship. Let the power of ancient altars be broken, in Jesus' name.

Awaken the Church in every nation from slumber. Awaken us, Lord, from sleep and spiritual dullness. Show us where we have slipped and fallen away or slept as the enemy has come to sow tares in our fields.

Lord, send angels to patrol my territory as the night progresses. I decree that tares will not be sown in my fields tonight. I plead the blood of Jesus over my life and my inheritance.

Let new networks of prayer be raised up that intercede for communities and nations according to Your will. I decree that these times of intercession will not be religious or legalistic. I decree that these will be times when the fire of the Lord is released from our lips to consume our enemies.

Let planned acts of terrorism against nations be exposed, in Jesus' name.

Lord, give me favor in every endeavor of my life. Give me favor to share the Gospel, and make me an example of righteousness so that others can be drawn to the Lord through my life.

Let favor surround me like a shield all the time. Let favor surround my city. I decree that the rate of violence is decreasing in my city.

Lord, cause the enemies of the Church in America to begin to promote God's prophetic purposes for the Church. Let the wineskin of religion that has veiled the church and distorted Your voice be broken now, and let the paradigm of the Church shift to reflect the forward-moving Kingdom.

I renounce every assignment of generational poverty in my life, in the name of Jesus.

I decree that the divine favor of God covers my life, in Jesus' name.

Lord, make my life a terror to my enemies. Turn me into untouchable coals of fire that are too hot for the enemy to handle.

Lord, You teach my hands to war and my fingers to fight (Psalm 144:1). Give me prophetic decrees that will begin to break every stronghold of the enemy in every area of my life, in the name of Jesus.

Let my enemies be put to shame, in Jesus' name.

Lord, I ask that You release what I need so that my need can be supplied. Open the door of business to me. Anoint me with creativity that brings wealth to me.

Let the fire of God begin to destroy every evil plan against any area of my life, in Jesus' name.

Lord, expose and disgrace all the schemes of Satan ever devised against me through any source and at any time.

I forsake every personal sin that has given ground to the enemy, in the name of Jesus.

I reclaim the ground that I have lost to the enemy. This is my season of retribution!

I command every spirit of infirmity to leave my life now, in Jesus' name. My next doctor's appointment will reflect healing.

I release creative miracles in every area of my life.

I command the spirit of destruction operating against me and my family, church and city to leave now. I call you off of your assignment, in Jesus' name.

Lord, take me from where I am to where You want me to be, in Jesus' name.

Lord, establish me in truth, godliness and faithfulness.

Lord, add favor, increase and profitability to my work. I reap a hundredfold increase on all of my labor.

I rebuke every anti-profit spirit attempting to operate against me. I am experiencing increase and abundance in every area of my life.

Lord, release the angels of heaven on my behalf to attack every Pharaonic system attempting to imprison me and my finances. I will no longer be held captive by poverty. Increase comes to me today and every day.

Lord, You fulfill the number of my days and satisfy my mouth with good things. Preserve my life from every assignment of premature death and destruction.

I decree that my children and grandchildren will walk in supernatural favor all the days of their lives. My children will possess the land.

My children will possess the gates of their enemies!

I decree that I walk in supernatural abundance, and there is no lack in my house. My children walk in supernatural abundance, and they have favor with God and with man.

Today and every day, God is plundering my oppressors; my house will lack no good thing. I decree that today and every day, I recognize my season of supernatural favor, and I will not miss my time.

I will walk in supernatural favor. As the dew falls upon Mount Hermon (Psalm 133:3), supernatural favor falls upon me.

I ask for turnarounds and breakthroughs.

Let every wall of resistance against me come down now, in Jesus' name!

God, according to 3 John 2, You desire that we would prosper spiritually, physically and materially. They that seek the Lord shall not want any good thing (Psalm 34:10).

Let all demonic forces holding my blessings be defeated, in the name of Jesus.

I send back to the sender every curse: poverty, lack, layoffs, lost jobs, family trouble, sickness, lack of church growth, lack of a building, broken marriages, financial trouble and rebellious children, as well as things not mentioned.

Let the spirit of delay and hindrance be cast out of my life today, in Jesus' name.

I reject the spirit of slavery and hard work for little pay or no pay, in Jesus' name. Beginning today, my labor will bring forth abundant provision for my life. I decree that I will not have labor without reward; I will eat the fruit of my labor.

I call every anti-breakthrough spirit off of your assignment, in Jesus' name!

I decree that there will not be compromise or dialogue between me and my enemies, in Jesus' name.

I plead the blood of Jesus over the spirit of Pisgah (delay). I decree that I will break through in every area of ministry and life. Beginning today, my life is going to the next level!

I rebuke every assignment of failure, in Jesus' name.

Let God arise and every enemy of my breakthrough be scattered.

I decree that I will not labor without reward!

Let the fire of God melt away every stone hindering my blessings, in Jesus' name.

Lord, do not let me carry any unprofitable or heavy load. Your yoke is easy and Your burden is light.

Lord, You satisfy my mouth with good things. Let Your satisfying portion be released to me today and everyday.

I refuse to be a seer of goodness without manifestation! I decree that this is my manifestation season!

Lord, let mega-blessings, mega-favor and mega-changes begin to happen in my life beginning today.

I command the release of every blessing timed for today; may they be released into my hands.

Lord, fill the cup of my life to the brim. I will not live my days in the earth unhappy. My life is filled with happiness and joy; my cup runs over.

Let every demonic force stopping my goodness receive God's arrow of fire now, in the name of Jesus!

I reject every spirit of the tail, in Jesus' name. I decree that the blessings of Deuteronomy 28:1–13 manifest in my life today and everyday.

I walk in the finishing anointing. I will finish this month strong. I will finish this year strong. I will finish my life strong.

You are Alpha and Omega; You will perfect everything that concerns me.

I command the powers of hell resisting me and my breakthrough to break now.

Lord, speedily avenge me upon my adversaries.

Lord, let me experience Your justice in every area of my life. Prepare a table for me in the presence of my enemies.

I cancel every ungodly delay to the manifestations of my miracles, in the name of Jesus.

I cancel every secret word of delay spoken over my life in the earth realm.

Lord, hasten over Your word to perform it in every area of my life.

Let there be turbulence, rearrangement, revision, reorganization and rerouting of situations and circumstances that are hindering the manifestation of my desired miracles, in Jesus' name.

I command the earth to yield enlarged territorial blessings to me, in Jesus' name.

I command creation to cooperate with me and not against me.

Lord, make my name great in the earth so that I can make Your name great.

Let properties and resources be given to me so that I can advance Your Kingdom in my region.

I plunder and render as nothing every anti-testimony, anti-miracle and anti-prosperity force working against me, in Jesus' name.

The God of Elijah who answers by fire is my God. Let Him who quickens and calls things that are not as though they are answer me by fire, in Jesus' name.

Let the fire of God be released against my enemies.

Let every plan and design of evil against my life be nullified, in Jesus' name.

I break myself loose from every assignment of stagnation, in Jesus' name.

Lord, let Your fire destroy anything that makes Your promises fail in my life.

I command all satanic networks against my fruitfulness to be completely broken, in the name of Jesus.

I thank You, Lord, for every good testimony that will come in the next seven days as a result of my prayers.

Lord, give me miracles that will astonish my enemies.

I break free from every limitation placed on my gifts and abilities. Let every demonic conspiracy against me be exposed. Every trap that has been set for me, my enemies will fall into. Every demonic confederacy operating against me is defeated today and every day, in Jesus' name.

21. THIRD WATCH OF THE NIGHT

12:00 MIDNIGHT TO 3:00 A.M.

This watch is a transitional watch that occurs when deep sleep falls upon man and demonic activity escalates. The devil operates during this watch because he knows that people are asleep and there are fewer awake to oppose him. This watch carries an anointing to operate in the Spirit of God to overrule ungodly decrees.

DISTINCTIONS OF THIS WATCH: TAKING AUTHORITY OVER THE ENEMY

- This watch is a time to overturn unrighteous structures and release judgment upon your enemies. The plague of death was released in Egypt at midnight, killing the firstborn among the Egyptians (Exodus 11–12). At midnight Samson took hold of the doors of the gate of Gaza, pulling up the gate and gateposts and carrying them away on his shoulders (Judges 16:3).

- In this watch we dismantle evil assignments in government and within the societal sphere. An anointing is released in this watch to possess the gates of your enemies in a new way.

- Great joy and anointing is released during this watch: "At midnight I will rise to give thanks to You, because of Your righteous judgments" (Psalm 119:62 NKJV).

- Ruth laid at the feet of Boaz in the field during this watch (Ruth 3:8). "And at midnight a cry was heard: 'Behold, the bridegroom is coming; go out to meet him!'" (Matthew 25:6 NKJV). Pray for marriages and relationships.

- The midnight watch is a time of careful watching (Mark 13:32–35) and a time to ask, seek and knock (Luke 11:5–13). Pray for deliverance from your enemies, as Paul and Silas did (Acts 16:25). You can operate in a deeper anointing to make your case in prayer during this watch.

> *Thou shalt not be afraid of the terror by night, nor of the arrow that flieth by day, nor of the pestilence that walketh in darkness, nor of the destruction that layeth waste at noonday. A thousand shall fall at thy side, and ten thousand at thy right hand, but it shall not come nigh thee. Only with thine eyes shalt thou behold and see the reward of the wicked. Because thou hast made the LORD, who is my refuge, even the Most High, thy habitation, there shall no evil befall thee, neither shall any plague come nigh thy dwelling. For He shall give His angels charge over thee to keep thee in all thy ways.*
>
> **PSALM 91:5–11**

- Because humans are often experiencing deeper levels of sleep, demonic thieves operate during this time. This is a time to arise and catch the thief who is attempting to operate in your field. Release judgment upon the thief and receive retribution, for when the thief is caught, he must restore your loss sevenfold (Proverbs 6:31). Multiplication and increase are a principle of restoration, not just receiving back what was lost or taken. Restoration includes retribution, the divine payback owed to you.

PRAYERS, DECREES AND CONFESSIONS

I speak peace to every situation of turbulence and confusion that is trying to overwhelm me.

Paul and Silas were released from prison and Samson carried the gates at midnight. I decree that I am being delivered from every prison tonight!

I ask for a greater level of concentration and focus so that I can effectively rule in the midst of my enemies.

I command every evil voice whispering in my life to be silenced, in the name of Jesus.

Let every evil host gathered against me be scattered and never regroup again, in the name of Jesus.

Let all anti-testimony forces fashioned against my life be scattered by the thunder of God. Let them never regroup against me, in the name of Jesus.

I rebuke every demonic confederacy attempting to operate against me, in Jesus' name.

I reject partial or temporary freedom; I declare that I am fully free, in Jesus' name.

I break the power of any demonic spell released against my life.

Every evil assignment preventing my miracles from manifesting, I call you off of your assignment.

Let my tongue become an instrument of glory, in Jesus' name.

Let my hands become instruments of divine prosperity, in Jesus' name.

Let my eyes become instruments of divine revelation, in Jesus' name.

I rebuke every agent of demonic delay, and I call you off of your assignment.

Every agent of demotion, delay, defeat, frustration, vexation and infirmity, I command you to cease all operation against me.

I go from glory to glory and from blessing to blessing. I do not go from grace to grass. My life is getting better every day.

Every agent of confusion, backwardness and failure, I call you off your assignment and command you to cease your operations against me, my family, my church and my city.

I command every scanner spirit, eavesdropping spirit and spirit bringing distortion of words that come to confuse my mind and bring chaos to leave, in Jesus' name.

I decree termination of any assignment of almost there, the edge of breakthrough or so close to a miracle.

I rebuke spirits of disappointment and hope deferred.

Let the effects of any evil attachment be nullified, in Jesus' name.

Lord, anoint my life to receive multiple blessings.

I reject every spirit of financial embarrassment. I rebuke every assignment of not having enough. I decree that abundance is flowing in my life today and every day.

I rebuke every God-robbing spirit attempting to operate against me, in Jesus' name.

I release myself from every family curse resulting from God-robbing that is reinforcing financial problems in my life.

Let all powers in possession of my finances release them now, in Jesus' name.

I stand against every dream of defeat, in Jesus' name.

I decree that every stone of reproach operating against me is defeated, in Jesus' name.

Every assignment of hell operating against me, my family and my ministry to bring embarrassment is defeated by the strong arm of the Lord today.

Lord, rend the heavens and reveal hidden treasures to me.

Lord, give me revelation that would advance my life.

Lord, let the anointing of holiness fall upon my life.

I possess the gates of the enemy today.

I decree and claim increased vision and wisdom today.

Lord, send Your angels to battle on my behalf.

I walk in divine safety and refuse to enter into any trap of the enemy.

Lord, be my hiding place and preserve me from evil in every area of my life.

Lord, surround me with songs of deliverance—and let me hear Your song.

I render all evil challenges over my life powerless, in the name of Jesus.

I send back fiery arrows from hell released against me, my family and my church.

Lord, let all strange fires prepared by the enemy, whether in the second heaven, on the earth or underneath the earth, be quenched, in Jesus' name.

Let every evil tongue issuing destruction against my life be condemned, in Jesus' name.

I bind every spirit of deception working against my life, in Jesus' name.

Lord, cleanse my mind of every painful and destructive thought, in Jesus' name.

I release myself from every serpentine bite and poison, in Jesus' name. I plead the blood of Jesus over my life and declare healing over every demonic wound I have ever received.

I command the spirit of python to uncoil from around me, my family, my church and my city, in Jesus' name.

I break the power of every evil ritual aimed at me.

I break the hold of any evil power over me.

I bind the spirit of the snail that keeps me from advancing in time.

I bind every spirit of delay and failure to progress.

I bind every stronghold operating in my life.

I command all curses issued against me to be smashed and broken, in the name of Jesus.

I receive total healing and restoration in my body.

I bind the strongman over my family, my church and my city, in the name of Jesus.

Let all evil friends make mistakes that would expose them.

Let the strongmen from both sides of my family begin to fight and destroy themselves.

Let the secrets of hidden and open enemies be revealed. Lord, reveal any Judas that is in my life.

Lord, walk back through every second of my life and make me whole in any area in which the spirit of trauma is hiding.

Lord, set me free from any generational sins and iniquities that are operating in me.

Lord, set me free from demonic assignments of rejection transferred to me in the womb.

Lord, set me free from any curse or evil dedication spoken over me at birth.

Lord, set me free from every superstition of veils covering my face at birth. I am not veiled, I am revealed. Every demonic hood that was over me at birth is broken now.

I fall out of agreement with every work of darkness operating in me and through me, in Jesus' name.

I release the *shamar* anointing over my life, in Jesus' name. Everything connected to me is marked by the blood of Jesus. I command everything that has been stolen from my life to be returned. I am in my season of retribution!

By the authority and power of the blood of Jesus, I command every thief operating in my life to return what was stolen from me and to pay sevenfold tribute to me.

The blood of Jesus is my shield against every power of darkness that would come against me.

I command every stubborn sin issue operating in my life to leave, in Jesus' name.

I am free from every captivity, in Jesus' name.

I command every wounded place in my soul to be healed by the power of the blood of Jesus.

I throw off every burden of worry, in Jesus' name. I receive the joy of the Lord today.

I will not be anxious for anything. I receive the peace of God today and every day.

I reverse any damage done to my life from birth, in Jesus' name.

I command every spirit holding my gifts captive to let go, in Jesus' name. I am fully functioning in my Kingdom identity.

Every vagabond spirit trying to operate in my life, I command you to leave. I am steadfast in the house of God, and I will not be uprooted.

I loose myself from any orphan spirit operating in my life, in Jesus' name.

I command the spirit of stagnation to leave my life, in Jesus' name.

I overcome by the blood of the Lamb and by the words of my testimony. I testify to the atmosphere that I am free, and whomever the Son of man sets free is really free.

I command every time waster to leave my life, in Jesus' name.

I send the judgment of the Lord upon every spirit of wickedness in the land. I decree the Word of God will be established in the land, resulting in freedom from injustice and every oppression. Lord, I decree punishment for the wicked in high places of the land. I decree that idols and evil forces in the land will receive their portion from the Lord.

Lord, let the angels of heaven intervene on my behalf.

Lord, according to Psalm 119:62, I thank You for life and for Your Word, which brings me hope each day.

Lord, move in my life, church, family, economy and government in a new way.

Lord, I thank You that I am awake now to pray for my family and territory.

I decree what is written in Psalm 68. Lord, arise and let every enemy of my purpose and destiny be scattered, according to Psalm 68:1.

Lord, I ask You to blow my enemies away like smoke. Let Your wind blow them away.

God, I ask You to smash the heads of Your enemies, according to Psalm 68:21.

Lord, I ask that You show me Your power, according to Psalm 68:28.

Lord, I thank You that all authority and leadership comes from You. Thank You for leaders in my family, church and nation who are citizens of Your Kingdom.

Lord, raise up a new generation of righteous leadership to lead my city and nation.

Awaken me out of sleep that I might see the thief who has come to steal, kill and destroy.

Lord, expose every area in which the enemy has stolen from me to prevent me from fulfilling my Kingdom mandate. Help me to walk in humility and repentance. Help me to return to my first love, the highest place of my calling.

Deliver me from every area in which I have been bound due to generational or personal sin issues.

Let the heavens declare the glory of God and give praises to God, since He created them for His pleasure. I command the heavens to ignore every other proclamation contrary to giving pleasure to, glorifying and praising God who created them, according to Psalms 50 and 89.

Lord, I thank You that I am a vessel who carries Your presence in my life.

Lord, I ask You to deliver me from spiritual drowsiness and spiritual sleep.

Lord, arrest every thief sent to steal from me. I ask that the thief would be exposed, caught and disgraced.

I command the thief to repay sevenfold what was taken from me. My restoration has not been completed until I have received retribution.

Let every residue of satanic structures established in my nation be discerned and destroyed.

Enlighten my spiritual eyes and give me access to spiritual gates established by the enemy in the land.

I decree that my marriage is getting better and better. My family will fulfill the purpose of God.

I command every spirit of jealousy, insecurity and covenant breaking attempting to operate against my marriage to leave now, in Jesus' name.

My family is healthy, strong and prosperous. We will not bite and devour each other.

I decree unity in my family. The peace of God abides in my family in a new way, in Jesus' name.

I break generational assignments of divorce that have plagued my bloodline, in Jesus' name.

Every curse that has been sent against my marriage, family, business, finances and health is returned to sender, in Jesus' name.

I command crop failure over every false word, false prophecy and demonic prediction, in Jesus' name.

Beginning today, my family is increasing in favor with God and man.

Every assignment of nightmares and night terrors that come to interrupt my dreams is broken now. My children are being delivered from nightmares and night terrors, in Jesus' name.

I activate dreams of creativity as I sleep.

As I sleep, fires will not break out and thieves will not break in, in Jesus' name.

Let the angels of the Lord encamp around my house each night. I command the death angel to bypass my house, in Jesus' name. I and my children will live the number of days planned for us by the Lord.

I will not be afraid of the terror by night. Any plan of destruction formed against me in the night season is defeated (Psalm 91:5–6).

Lord, I thank You that Your love is redemptive. Your love for me caused You to secure salvation for the world through the shed blood of Jesus.

22. FOURTH WATCH OF THE NIGHT

3:00 A.M. TO 6:00 A.M.

This watch is referred to as the dawn or early morning watch. Significant aspects of this watch are deliverance, resurrection and a release of God's will on earth as it is in heaven. There is an anointing to reorder the day ahead of you, nullifying demonic operations planned against you. During this watch we decree God's judgments against the wicked.

DISTINCTIONS OF THIS WATCH: RELEASING THE LIGHT

- The Lord overthrew the Egyptians in the midst of the sea during the morning watch (Exodus 14:24–28). This is a time to release judgment against evil assignments, for God says He will destroy the wicked in the land at that time of the day: "Early I will destroy all the wicked of the land, that I may cut off all the evildoers from the city of the LORD" (Psalm 101:8 NKJV).

- Demonic powers heighten their activities between the hours of midnight and 3:00 a.m., knowing that by the early morning watch, they will have to cease their activities so that they will not be caught by the intensity of the dayspring (that is, the break of dawn). Occult practitioners operate during the night, casting spells, hexes and vexes, incantations, etc. This is a time to release judgment against the wicked who remain stiff-necked and unrepentant. They have received many warning and rebukes but refuse to repent. "He who hardens his neck and refuses instruction after being often reproved (corrected, criticized), will suddenly be broken beyond repair" (Proverbs 29:1 AMP).

- "Those who take, take, take will come to nothing and run away" (Isaiah 17:14 VOICE). God has promised to protect you and to release His judgment against your enemies.

- You can also release God's rebuke upon your enemies during this watch.

> *The nations shall rush like the rushing of many waters; but God shall rebuke them, and they shall flee far off, and shall be chased as the chaff of the mountains before the wind and like a rolling thing before the whirlwind. And behold, at eventide, trouble; and before the morning, he is no more. This is the portion of them that despoil us, and the lot of them that rob us.*
>
> **ISAIAH 17:13–14**

> *O house of David, thus says the* LORD: *"Administer justice in the morning, and rescue the one who has been robbed from the hand of his oppressor, that My wrath will not roar up like fire and burn so [hotly] that none can extinguish it, because of the evil of their deeds."*
>
> **JEREMIAH 21:12 AMP**

- During this watch, we command the morning. "Since your days began, have you ever commanded the morning, and caused the dawn to know its place, so that light may take hold of the corners of the earth and shake the wickedness out of it?" (Job 38:12–13 AMP).

- The early morning watch is a time to release your sacrifice of prayer unto the Lord. Jesus is our pattern, who often prayed early in the morning, long before the breaking of dawn.

- It is a time to pray for the new day to open unto you. "Your gates will always be open. They will not be closed, day or night. Nations and kings will bring their wealth to you" (Isaiah 60:11 ERV).

- We can count on the Lord to deliver us from storms, as Jesus came walking on the water during this watch to deliver the disciples from the heavy winds: "And in the fourth watch of the night, Jesus went unto them, walking on the sea" (Matthew 14:25).

- This is also the time the stone before Jesus' tomb was rolled away. Every reproach must be rolled away at this hour. As resurrection power was manifested during this watch, expect to see the resurrection of every dormant gift.

> *At the end of the Sabbath, as it began to dawn toward the first day of the week, came Mary Magdalene and the other Mary to see the sepulcher. And behold, there was a great earthquake, for the angel of the Lord descended from Heaven, and came and rolled back the stone from the door, and sat upon it.*
>
> **MATTHEW 28:1–2**

- Finally, this watch heralds the emergence of the dawn. It is a time to release the light of the Lord.

> *I, Jesus, have sent Mine angel to testify unto you these things in the churches. I am the Root and the Offspring of David, and the Bright and Morning Star.*
>
> **REVELATION 22:16**

> *We have also a more sure word of prophecy, unto which ye do well that ye take heed, as unto a light that shineth in a dark place, until the day dawn and the day star arise in your hearts.*
>
> **2 PETER 1:19**

Arise, shine, for thy light is come, and the glory of the LORD *is risen upon thee. For behold, the darkness shall cover the earth and gross darkness the people; but the* LORD *shall arise upon thee, and His glory shall be seen upon thee. And the Gentiles shall come to thy light, and kings to the brightness of thy rising. Lift up thine eyes round about and see; all they gather themselves together, they come to thee; thy sons shall come from far, and thy daughters shall be nursed at thy side. Then thou shalt see and flow together, and thine heart shall fear and be enlarged, because the abundance of the sea shall be converted unto thee, the wealth of the Gentiles shall come unto thee.*

ISAIAH 60:1–5

PRAYERS, DECREES AND CONFESSIONS

Lord, I take authority over this day, in Jesus' name.

I decree that every resource I need to be successful and victorious today is released to me.

I confess that this is the day the Lord has made, and I will rejoice and be glad in it.

Lord, raise up a standard against every enemy that has arisen to attack me and my family, church, city and nation, in Jesus' name. Let every plan and strategy of the enemy against me today be defeated in the same way You defeated the chariots of Egypt.

Lord, release the full intensity of the daybreak (dayspring) to grab hold of the ends of the earth and shake out every wicked assignment against the purposes of my life, family, church and nation. Expose every assignment of evil against me for what it really is.

Everything that has died in terms of my potential, in the **PART II** church and in the nation, is receiving resurrection power of the Lord. Every gift in me that should be active now is receiving resurrection power, in the name of Jesus.

I render null and void every hex, vex, incantation, curse or utterance against me, in Jesus' name.

I decree that every assignment formed against me during the night will fail.

Those who spent the night pulling me down are pulled down themselves. I rise higher and higher, and my life is getting better and better. I prosper today, in Jesus' name.

I decree that every reproach in my life is rolled away, in Jesus' name.

Holy Spirit, awaken me and other Kingdom citizens in my territory early to pray and invoke divine judgments of God on every work of wickedness that takes place during this watch.

Holy Spirit, awaken me every day with a song of praise in my heart. Awaken me from spiritual slumber.

Holy Spirit, train my hands for war and my fingers for battle so that I can contend with the wickedness that is actively released at this time of night.

Lord, help me to renew my mind so that I can meditate on the Word of the Lord. I ask that the Holy Spirit bring light to my eyes and revival to my soul, according to Psalm 19:7–11.

Lord, release Your angels to roll back every stone of limitation and bondage in my family and the nation. Let the prodigals in my family hear Your voice calling them to return to You.

Lord, I pray that the Church will arise and shine so that God's purposes will be accomplished in our nation.

Lord, give the Church an understanding of how Your economy works. Help the Church to understand how we freely receive and how we are to freely give.

Lord, I ask that You bless me. Let blessings flow into my life from heaven.

Lord, bless the economy of our nation. Let there be supernatural turnaround of financial deficits that lead to poverty in families, in Jesus' name.

Let nations repent for fostering false worship systems resulting in financial curses. Let nations turn to the true and living God.

I rebuke assignments of greed, theft and corruption contributing to the financial oppression of the citizens of the nation.

Let nations begin to operate in the economy of heaven.

Let unseen blessings be released unto me. Let me receive hidden treasures of wealth that now reside in darkness. Let sudden financial blessings overtake me.

Let me receive blessings that generations in my family before me did not walk in.

I decree that the blood of Jesus cleanses me from any legal ground the enemy has against me.

Let the strongholds and seat of the enemy in my life be abolished, in the name of Jesus.

Let the anointing of the overcomer be released to overflowing in my life.

I overcome every assignment of poverty and command poverty to leave my life.

I overcome every assignment of frustration, vexation, fear and unbelief. I command these assignments to leave my life.

Lord, shake the wickedness out of the heavens over me, and let the day ahead be filled with blessings, glory, favor, health, honor and prosperity.

I decree that wealth, riches, favor, prosperity and health are established in my house, in the name of Jesus.

I pray that the power of the blood of Jesus is released against all satanic covenants with the grave; my resources will be released.

Lord, raise up strong men and strong women to pray that the dayspring takes the earth by the edges and shakes out all the wicked structures in the nations' economic systems.

Let every wicked structure keeping the world's wealth in the hands of 1 percent of the world's population be pulled down now.

Lord, I ask that You rend the heavens and come down, causing favor, power, promotion, breakthrough, finances, good health, sound mind and peace to be released into my life.

> *There is no one like the LORD our God. He sits on his throne high in heaven...He lifts the poor out of the dirt and rescues beggars from the garbage dump. He puts them in important positions, giving them a place among the leaders of his people.*
>
> **PSALM 113:5, 7–8 ERV**

God has spoken over my life; I believe it and I begin to manifest it. I am not a failure. I shall operate as the head only and not the tail. The assignment of the tail is broken off of my life. I shall dwell on the mountains only and not in the valley; I shall no longer experience the activities of the spirit of Pisgah (delay).

I shall no longer be disappointed or fail at the edge of my desired miracles, success and victory, for the blood of Jesus has delivered my life from every assignment of witchcraft, hatred, jealousy and envy.

I have been given authority over every assignment of evil; today and every day, I trample under my feet every serpent of treachery, wicked schemes and plots against me, evil reports, accusation and criticism. No counsel of the wicked shall stand against me. God is for me; who can stand against me? I declare that victory after victory manifests in my life today and every day.

No weapon formed against me shall prosper, and every tongue that rises up against me is already condemned. Therefore, I tear down in faith every spiritual wall of petition between me and my divinely appointed helpers and benefactors. Let everyone assigned by God, who is the King of the universe, bless my life today.

I stand in my position as a child of God, ordained to reign as a king on earth. I decree the divine favor of God fills me. God has put His Word in my mouth as a weapon of destruction and restoration. I use that power to speak destruction upon all the devil's agents assigned to hinder me and divert my blessings. I use the same weapon to decree restoration upon my life.

I decree that any assignment from hell that has been operating against God's purpose in and for my life, community, family and church is being arrested by the angel of the Lord.

I pray that God's original blueprint for man will be fully restored. I pray for the restoration of dominion over creation, as God intended. I pray that I will walk in dominion in every area of life, as God intended.

I decree that tonight Jesus will rise and shine in my life, heart, ministry, family, city, region and nation as the bright and morning Star (Revelation 22:16). Lord, I ask You to arise in greater measure and degree. I open my heart and say, "Arise, O Lord, in me!"

I cancel every assignment of the dragon, including all the words (waters) he has poured forth out of his mouth to flood me, my family, my city, my community and my nation.

I pray that the earth will open its mouth and swallow up all of the waters the dragon has spewed out to flood me.

Then the dragon poured water out of its mouth like a river. It poured the water toward the woman so that the flood would carry her away. But the earth helped the woman. The earth opened its mouth and swallowed the river that came from the mouth of the dragon.

REVELATION 12:15–16 ERV

I command the stars in heaven to reflect the bright and morning star, Jesus! Creation will not operate against me. Creation will speak forth the praises of God, and there is no speech nor language in which its voice will not be heard.

Lord, I thank You that this is not only the day You have made but the day of multiplication, replenishing abundance and subduing all things under Your rule. Holy Spirit, I ask You to teach me and my family how to make Your values a reality in our day-to-day, walking-around life.

Lord, I thank You that You are love. There is no other love that can be as complete as the love of God. I pray that Your love will be made manifest more and more in the relationships of every Kingdom citizen in my territory, starting with me.

It is written that I should not consider the former things, for God shall do a new thing in my life, and it shall speedily spring forth (Isaiah 43:18–19). I ask that new things begin to spring forth in my marriage, my business and finances, my ministry and my spiritual life.

The Lord will make His face to shine upon me always and shall be gracious unto me. His light will shine on my path, and His favor will encompass me all the days of my life.

My confessions are covered in the blood of Jesus and manifest in my life today.

23. First Watch of the Day

6:00 A.M. to 9:00 A.M.

God is known for being a covenant keeper. Throughout biblical history, God has established and kept covenant with humans and His creation. Scripture reveals God's covenant with day and night: "If ye can break My covenant of the day and My covenant of the night, and that there should not be day and night in their season…" (Jeremiah 33:20).

God's covenant with day and night establishes the sequence of their appearances. Day and night appear only at their proper times, never at the wrong time. Nor can God's covenant with the day be broken (Jeremiah 33:25–26).

> *Thus saith the LORD, who giveth the sun for a light by day, and the ordinances of the moon and of the stars for a light by night, who divideth the sea when the waves thereof roar; the LORD of hosts is His name: "If those ordinances depart from before Me," saith the LORD, "then the seed of Israel also shall cease from being a nation before Me for ever."*
> **JEREMIAH 31:35–36**

The first watch of the day begins with sunrise, and we experience the power of the Son rising upon us as we begin our day. When we awaken in the first watch, we release decrees and prayers that set the day ahead in Kingdom order.

At each and every sunrise you will hear my voice as I prepare my sacrifice of prayer to you. Every morning I lay out the pieces of my life on the altar and wait for your fire to fall upon my heart.

PSALM 5:3 PASSION

DISTINCTIONS OF THIS WATCH: RISING SON OF RIGHTEOUSNESS

- The first watch of the day is a time to believe that Jesus, the King of kings and Lord of lords, will rise over us. "But unto you that fear My name shall the Sun of Righteousness arise with healing in His wings; and ye shall go forth and grow up as calves from the stall" (Malachi 4:2). This a time to ask the Lord to release His voice throughout your day, in every circumstance. As you enter your day, receive God's restorative power in your life.

- The beginning of each day is a time to appropriate the benefits of redemption, which include restoration and healing. Because we ask the Son of righteousness to arise with healing in His wings, any area of our lives that is broken or wounded, whether physically or financially, can be healed during this time. Decrees for healing of body, mind, soul, heart, emotions, families, relationships, marriages and the land can be powerfully effective in the first watch.

- Students prepare for the day ahead in the educational system during this watch. Prayers for this gate of society can be offered at this time, including prayers for your children as they begin their day in school. Pray for teachers and other students with whom your children will interact. Ask the Lord to overturn any unrighteous practices that might be occurring in the educational system.

- The Holy Spirit was poured out on the disciples for the first time during this watch. Pray for the outpouring of the Holy Spirit in your life, asking the Lord to teach you how to operate in the supernatural realm with power and authority. Decree that each word you speak throughout the day will be marked by the fire and presence of the Lord.

> *And when the day of Pentecost was fully come, they were all with one accord in one place. And suddenly there came a sound from heaven as of a rushing mighty wind, and it filled all the house where they were sitting. And there appeared unto them cloven tongues as of fire, and it sat upon each of them. And they were all filled with the Holy Ghost and began to speak in other tongues, as the Spirit gave them utterance...."These are not drunken as ye suppose, seeing it is but the third hour of the day."*
>
> **ACTS 2:1–4, 15**

- Ask the Lord to give you seeing eyes and hearing ears. As you enter your day, you need fresh revelation. Anoint your eyes and ears and declare that you will see and hear today and every day. Ask the Lord to release the seer anointing upon you so that you can see in the spirit realm.

> *The Lord GOD hath given Me the tongue of the learned, that I should know how to speak a word in season to him that is weary. He wakeneth morning by morning; He wakeneth Mine ear to hear as the learned. The Lord GOD hath opened Mine ear, and I was not rebellious, neither turned away back.*
>
> **ISAIAH 50:4–5**

- The first watch is a time for the voice of the Lord to be released with power and might. Invite the voice of the Lord to be released throughout your day. Decree that every voice of the enemy will be silenced by the voice of the Lord.

> *The LORD also shall roar out of Zion, and utter His voice from Jerusalem, and the heavens and the earth shall shake; but the LORD will be the hope of His people, and the strength of the children of Israel.*
>
> **JOEL 3:16**

> *At the brightness that was before Him, His thick clouds passed, hail stones and coals of fire. The LORD also thundered in the heavens, and the Highest uttered His voice with hail stones and coals of fire. Yea, He sent out His arrows and scattered them; and He shot out lightnings and discomfited them.*
>
> **PSALM 18:12–14**

- The first watch is also a time for the justice of God to be released. God is our righteous judge. Invite Him to overturn unrighteous decisions affecting you and your family, your city and your nation.

> *I will early destroy all the wicked of the land, that I may cut off all wicked doers from the city of the LORD.*
>
> **PSALM 101:8**

> *This their way is their folly, yet their posterity approve their sayings. Selah. Like sheep they are laid in the grave; death shall feed on them, and the upright shall have dominion over them in the morning, and their beauty shall be consumed in the grave away from their dwelling.*
>
> **PSALM 49:13–14**

- As the sun rises and light overcomes the darkness of night, the first watch becomes a time for fresh joy and renewed hope to be released in your life. Time progresses in God's order from night to day. "Weeping may endure for a night, but joy cometh in the morning" (Psalm 30:5). Decree that as your day begins, expectation and hope will be renewed within you.

> *I awaited the dawning of the morning and cried; I hoped in Thy word. Mine eyes awaited the night watches, that I might meditate on Thy word. Hear my voice according unto Thy lovingkindness; O Lord, quicken me according to Thy judgment.*
>
> **Psalm 119:147–149**

Prayers, Decrees and Confessions

I declare that as the sun rises today, I will experience the goodness of the Lord. Creation will cooperate with me in the fulfillment of my destiny. As I labor with heaven today, the earth will yield everything that I need to be successful.

As the sun rises today, the Son of righteousness, Jesus Christ, is arising within me and on my behalf, bringing healing for my soul, heart, emotions, mind, body, family, relationships and marriage. I will experience healing in my prayer life, health, relationships, family, government and economy.

I decree a new outpouring of the Holy Spirit in my life, in my family, in my ministry and in my city, in Jesus' name.

Lord, give me songs of deliverance and joyful songs of love and praise as I prepare for this day.

Lord, give me listening ears, seeing eyes, a discerning spirit and a comprehending mind this morning and every morning.

Renew Your mercy toward me and my family, church and nation each morning. Lord, be my portion today.

Lord, I thank You that Your times and seasons will be constant as long as the earth remains, because You have made covenant with the day, according to Genesis 9 and Jeremiah 33:25–26.

Lord, I decree that my times and seasons are in Your hands and only Your hands.

This is the day that the Lord has made; I will rejoice and be glad in it. Today belongs to the Lord, and only His purposes will stand.

According to Job 38:12, Psalm 19:1–6 and Psalm 91, I speak into my day and command that the sun will not smite me today. Creation cooperates with my destiny today. Creation will bless me. The land will yield to me everything I need. There is no lack or want in my house.

Creation agrees with God and declares goodness over me, my family, my church and my city. I command creation to do only what God has purposed today. Only God's purposes will stand in my life.

Creation will not cooperate with the powers of hell against me. This is my season of mega-goodness and mega-mercy. Today I will receive gifts, surprises, checks in the mail, lost money found and bonanzas.

Lord, I ask that You speak today and silence every other voice that speaks into the day.

Lord, I thank You that weeping only last for a night, and joy comes in the morning. Let the dawning of my new day bring joy and newness of life and hope.

According to Genesis 49:27, the Lord is empowering me to overcome every evil force set against me today. As the morning watch breaks, I will overcome every obstacle set against me to hinder God's purpose in my life. As this new day comes into fullness, every obstacle set against my family, church and city to hinder God's purposes is overturned.

As the new day approaches, I will divide the plunder of the enemy in any areas he has stolen from me and my family, church and city. I decree that retribution is my portion, and I recover more than was taken from me.

Lord, I ask that You dispense justice on the unrighteous who refuse to put their trust in You. I decree that God will cause me to rule over the unrighteous and their followers. God is my salvation as the morning rises.

Lord, according to Matthew 6:11 and Psalm 5:1–3, today I lay my personal requests at Your feet, and I know that You will answer me.

I decree that my children will be instructed by the Lord concerning every area of their lives. Lord, surround my children with godly teachers who can instruct them and show them Your way.

Lord, I ask that You visit the education system in my city. Let godly teachers come to my child's school. I expose every assignment of humanism that would turn my child away from You; it will not stand. Let righteous lawmakers change unrighteous procedures in the educational system.

Let the anointing of wisdom, knowledge and understanding rest on my children, grandchildren and great-grandchildren. As Daniel and Joseph prospered in government, let my children walk in an anointing to rule with wisdom and honor wherever they go.

Lord, I pray that every pedophile and molester working or volunteering in my child's school and in schools throughout this city and nation be exposed, in the name of Jesus.

Lord, raise up godly curriculum writers. Let curricula with redemptive purposes be created.

Let every gift needed for me to achieve success today be activated **PART II** in me right now.

In every area where I am weak, You are equipping me to be effective.

My youth is renewed today, and every gate of hell is shut out of my life. The breath of the Lord is filling my heart right now, and He is strengthening my bones, according to Job 32:7–8 and Isaiah 58:11.

Lord, dispatch Your angels to roll away every stone preventing me from moving forward in life. Dispatch Your angels to roll away every stumbling block to my promotion, advancement and elevation.

I bind every strongman delegated to hinder my advancement and breakthrough, in the name of Jesus. I decree that my life is shifting to the next level God has planned for me, in Jesus' name.

Let every good and perfect gift that is from above locate me today.

I command the rain of abundance, goodness, favor and mercy to fall on every area of my life, in Jesus' name. I rebuke every assignment of dryness from my life.

I decree that today Kingdom citizens will willingly offer their bodies as instruments of righteousness and as laborers in the harvest.

Holy Spirit, be my companion today. Let a fresh anointing come upon me right now as I pray. Holy Spirit, counsel, uphold, warn and help me in all of my daily activities. Prompt me today when I forget You, and bring me back to the place of dependence on You in every moment of my life.

Teach me to walk gently with the Holy Spirit so that I do not grieve Him.

Strengthen my resolve to be faithful so I can enjoy the benefit of dwelling with God always.

24. SECOND WATCH OF THE DAY

9:00 A.M. TO 12:00 NOON

God has an appointed time for the manifestation of His promises. The second watch of the day is a time to pray for understanding of God's time and order. You should spend time asking the Lord to manifest His promises to you. Reading over previous prophetic words and declaring them aloud activate deeper measures of faith within you. There is also an anointing of faith that the Lord will release forgiveness and healing of broken relationships. This hour was when Jesus was crucified. Jesus chose obedience, and the second watch is a time to align your heart in obedience to the will of the Lord.

DISTINCTIONS OF THIS WATCH: GOD'S PROMISES MANIFESTED

- In Scripture, God promises to accomplish His Word. This is a time to remind God of His promises to you. "Put Me in remembrance; let us plead together; declare thou, that thou mayest be justified" (Isaiah 43:26). Prophecy is a promise from God. Spend time listening to or reading prophecies spoken over your life previously or reviewing prophetic dreams given to you by the Holy Spirit. Ask the Lord to give you revelation of whether you are in a waiting season or experiencing delay. Let the Lord show you what He is developing in you as you wait.

For as the heavens are higher than the earth, so are My ways higher than your ways and My thoughts than your thoughts. For as the rain cometh down and the snow from heaven, and returneth not thither, but watereth the earth, and maketh it bring forth and bud, that it may give seed to the sower and bread to the eater, so shall My word be that goeth forth out of My mouth: It shall not return unto Me void, but it shall accomplish that which I please, and it shall prosper in the thing whereto I sent it.

ISAIAH 55:9–11

Can a woman forget her sucking child, that she should not have compassion on the son of her womb? Yea, they may forget, yet will I not forget thee. Behold, I have graven thee upon the palms of My hands; thy walls are continually before Me.

ISAIAH 49:15–16

- Because the third watch is the time to arise in expectation to see God's promises to you manifested, ask the Lord to cleanse your heart from everything that does not please His heart. Pray for personal cleansing and deliverance. "Draw nigh to God, and He will draw nigh to you. Cleanse your hands, ye sinners, and purify your hearts, ye doubleminded" (James 4:8). Ask the Lord to forgive you for any doubt, unbelief or frustration that you may have yielded to; this is a time for deliverance from any doublemindedness you might have come into agreement with.

Therefore, brethren, we are debtors, not to the flesh to live according to the flesh; for if ye live according to the flesh ye shall die, but if ye through the Spirit do mortify the deeds of the body ye shall live. For as many as are led by the Spirit of God, they are the sons of God. For ye have not received the spirit of bondage again to fear, but ye have received the Spirit of adoption, whereby we cry, "Abba! Father!"

ROMANS 8:12–15

- This is a time to effectively pray for restoration, healing, reconciliation of relationships and forgiveness. Jesus taught forgiveness as a prerequisite of seeing our prayers answered (Mark 11:24–26), for unforgiveness blocks answers to prayer. Unforgiveness, when not dealt with, can become a root of bitterness. It is important to submit every aspect of your life to the Lord, allowing Him to deal with injustices committed against you.

> *Then shall thy light break forth as the morning, and thine health shall spring forth speedily; and thy righteousness shall go before thee; the glory of the LORD shall be thy rearward.*
>
> **ISAIAH 58:8**

> *He restoreth my soul; He leadeth me in the paths of righteousness for His name's sake.*
>
> **PSALM 23:3**

> *"For I will restore health unto thee, and I will heal thee of thy wounds," saith the LORD, "because they called thee an outcast, saying, "This is Zion, whom no man seeketh after."*
>
> **JEREMIAH 30:17**

> *After that He put His hands again upon his eyes and made him look up; and he was restored, and saw every man clearly.*
>
> **MARK 8:25**

- Prayers for harvest and increase can also be effective at this time. Increase and multiplication are Kingdom concepts. In the Garden, for example, Adam and Eve were instructed to increase and multiply. God's desire is that the whole earth would be filled with the knowledge of the glory of God (Habakkuk 2:14). Therefore, ask the Lord to raise up harvesters in your region. Ask Him to give you a burden for the harvest and send you forth as a harvester.

> *Let the people praise Thee, O God; let all the people praise Thee. Then shall the earth yield her increase; and God, even our own God, shall bless us. God shall bless us, and all the ends of the earth shall fear Him.*
>
> **PSALM 67:5–7**

- It was at this time of day that Jesus was crucified. Jesus chose obedience to the will of the Father. Ask the Lord to help you choose obedience, allowing Him to show you unsubmitted areas of your life and submitting what He shows you to Him. Pray for the power of a crucified life within you.

> *I am crucified with Christ, nevertheless I live; yet not I, but Christ liveth in me. And the life which I now live in the flesh, I live by the faith of the Son of God, who loved me and gave Himself for me.*
>
> **GALATIANS 2:20**

- Decrees concerning productivity in life and ministry are also effective at this time. Ask the Lord to help you to discern between Kingdom productivity and busyness. Allow Him to show you time wasters operating in your life and stealing your time. Ask the Lord to show you how to redeem time.

> *And when he had agreed with the laborers for a penny a day, he sent them into his vineyard. And he went out about the third hour and saw others standing idle in the marketplace.*
>
> **MATTHEW 20:2–3**

PRAYERS, DECREES AND CONFESSIONS

I come into agreement with Romans 8:12–15. I owe the flesh nothing. I crucify my flesh today. Today and every day I will submit to the leading of Holy Spirit.

Lord, baptize me with spiritual joy so I can give You continuous praise from my lips.

Holy Spirit, You are the Lord of the harvest. Raise up more laborers in the vineyard in my city so we can reach the lost who are seeking direction. Increase the level of our burden for evangelism.

Lord, continue to reveal the strategy of evangelism required to reach every people group, including youth, adults and senior citizens. Give me the courage to share my faith across ethnic and socioeconomic boundaries.

Lord, help me to be teachable today so that I can see the new thing You are doing. I will not resist new methods and new strategies for evangelism. Help me to be sensitive to Your voice.

Lord, You resist the proud, but You give grace to the humble. Help me to walk in humility today so that You can lift me up in honor. Let me walk in the spirit of meekness today sufficient to the challenges that will confront me.

I pray for those who are heavy laden, those carrying burdens, those who are depressed. I pray that today they will look to You for help.

I pray for the gate of science and technology. Release a new level of creativity within our educational system. Raise up a new generation of researchers and biologists from minority communities. Let there be a superabundance of witty inventions released through minority communities. Their ideas will not be stolen, and they will not be taken advantage of!

Lord, I thank You that new cures for cancer are being discovered. Let Your Spirit of revelation rest upon medical researchers, allowing them to see what they have not been able to see before.

Let new cures for incurable diseases be discovered.

Lord, let there be new cures for cancer that utilize nature.

Lord, I rebuke the spirit of greed that holds medicinal cures hostage, preventing the poor from having access.

Lord, I rebuke assignments of wickedness attempting to operate through the medical profession by prescribing unnecessary medicines to children. Let these assignments and operations be exposed.

I thank You for godly doctors and researchers who operate with great care and integrity for their patients.

Lord, let there be an increase of hospitals who care for children suffering from diseases like cancer.

Let various cunning inventions that You ordained to be founded in our nation be released.

I decree that any area would be exposed in which science and technology are being used to bring destruction rather than improvement in my nation. Lord, raise up people that create policies that protect the nations from destructive science and technology. I decree that hell will not operate through the gate of technology.

Let those who are gifted in science and technology but remain unknown due to poverty, racism or ignorance be uncovered. Let them be discovered! This is the season, Lord, that You will create a way by which their potential will be harnessed, to the glory of Your name. Show the Church how to operate and assist in this gate.

Today, I will continue to experience the resurrection power of Christ.

Show me areas in which the spirit of selfishness might be operating through my flesh. Holy Spirit, help me to crucify my selfish nature as I grow in You.

Lord, reveal any areas of woundedness that need healing, especially in the area of relationships.

Lord, bless the work of my hands. I pray for employment so that I can enjoy the blessing You have already put in my hands.

I decree that today the Word of God has an entrance into my life and releases me from bondage.

I decree in accordance with Psalm 119:30 that I have chosen to be loyal to You. I respect Your laws and Your ways.

I decree Psalm 36:10: Lord, continue to love those who really know You, and do good to those who are true to You.

Thank You for the grace to die to the flesh and the world so I can begin to live out John 12:24 and Galatians 2:20.

25. THIRD WATCH OF THE DAY

12:00 NOON TO 3:00 P.M.

The midnight and noon watches are significant because they represent transition. Spiritual activity increases around the time of these watches, culminating in a fullness of events.

> *And they took the bullock which was given them, and they dressed it, and called on the name of Baal from morning even until noon, saying, "O Baal, hear us!" But there was no voice, nor any that answered. And they leaped upon the altar which was made.*
>
> *And it came to pass at noon that Elijah mocked them and said, "Cry aloud, for he is a god! Either he is talking, or he is pursuing, or he is on a journey, or perhaps he sleepeth and must be awakened."*

1 KINGS 18:26–27

DISTINCTIONS OF THIS WATCH: SHAKING OF FOUNDATIONS

- This watch is a time to ask the Lord to allow righteousness to shine brighter and brighter like the sun (Psalm 37:3–6). As your righteousness shines brighter, those who do not know the Lord will be drawn to Him.

- During this watch, Peter had a powerful encounter with the Lord when he went to the rooftop to pray: "The next day they were coming near Joppa about noon, when Peter was going up to the roof to pray" (Acts 10:9 ERV). He fell into a trance, during which the Holy Spirit revealed God's plans to bring salvation to the Gentiles. Ask the Lord to show you people from other nations who need to hear the Gospel. Be faithful to pray for the nations the Lord shows you.

- Ask the Lord to give you revelation of heaven's activity. Saul of Tarsus experienced a supernatural meeting with heaven that brought him to salvation during this watch: "And it came to pass that, as I made my journey and had come nigh unto Damascus about noon, suddenly there shone from heaven a great light round about me" (Acts 22:6). Ask the Lord to let the eyes of your understanding be opened to comprehend spiritual things.

- This is a key time of day when assignments of destruction are released from the enemy. During this watch, ask the Lord to show you any demonic arrows that have been released against you. Ask Him to help you dwell in the secret place of His presence. Spend time thanking the Lord for His protection.

Evening and morning and at noon will I pray and cry aloud, and He shall hear my voice.

PSALM 55:17

Thou shalt not be afraid of the terror by night, nor of the arrow that flieth by day, nor of the pestilence that walketh in darkness, nor of the destruction that layeth waste at noonday. A thousand shall fall at thy side, and ten thousand at thy right hand, but it shall not come nigh thee.

PSALM 91:5–7

PRAYERS, DECREES AND CONFESSIONS

Lord, I thank You that I do not have to pray at designated times but can pray at any time.

As the day progresses, my righteousness will shine brighter and brighter. The pattern of my life will be one of moving from glory to glory.

I am going from grace to grace, higher and higher, rather than following the pattern of the kingdom of darkness, which is a rising and falling, from grace to grass.

I decree that the spirit of getting better and better will follow me in my endeavors.

Lord, give me the ability to multiply and replenish rather than deplete resources; this is the pattern You gave in the Garden of Eden. I am to be fruitful and multiply.

Everything I touch gets better and better. My life, health, children, family, church, city and finances get better and better.

I come into agreement with the Word of the Lord, which declares, "The path of those who live right is like the early morning light. It gets brighter and brighter until the full light of day" (Proverbs 4:18 ERV).

"I speak to God morning, noon, and night. I tell him what upsets me, and he listens to me!" (Psalm 55:17 ERV).

Destruction is released at midday (Psalm 91:6–7). I decree that every satanic arrow is being cut off now by the sword of the Lord as I pray.

I decree that God is delivering my soul in peace from the battle that was against me, according to Psalm 55:18.

I decree that justice is released on my behalf as I pray, because Emmanuel is with me (Isaiah 7:14).

I decree that at the fullness of this day, I will also see the fullness of my potential that God purposed for me to walk in.

What God purposed for me to achieve today will not be lost. I repent for wasting time. Holy Spirit, help me to redeem time.

Lord, continue to cover and protect me as the day continues. No pestilence that strikes at noonday will come near me or my family.

Lord, thank You for preserving me. Thank You that as my enemies arise, You will scatter them.

Lord, You are the foundation of my day; be also the climax of my day. Where I have been lost in the busyness and cares of the world, help me to come back to a place of meditating on Your goodness. I will find time to read Scriptures that help me to praise You. I join with creation to praise You!

I command the heavens to yield their best for me at this time. I pray that the favor of God will reach out to every area of my life, family and ministry.

I will remain in the secret place of the Most High God in the midst of the business of the day. Holy Spirit, draw me even nearer to You and guide me as I approach the closing of the day.

God, illuminate my horizon. Let the rays of God's powerful light introduce new ideas, new perceptions and new methods of doing things after the order of the Word of God.

At this time of day, my spiritual reflexes will be so opened to God that I can hear very clearly from Him.

God, confront the forces of tradition in the Body of Christ that have made the Word of God of no effect.

Today every believer that has been plundered or taken captive in any area of life is set free. God, release them from imprisonment.

Today I receive the grace to finish every project started under God or by the order or instruction of God.

I receive the faithfulness of spirit necessary to continue the race consistently to the end. There will no longer be abandoned or uncompleted projects, and I will not be subject to the "near" achievement syndrome that causes me to almost complete what I start without ever experiencing the reality.

Lord, I agree with Psalm 103:19 that declares Your throne is established in heaven and You rule over all other thrones and kings on the earth.

I pray that I will possess every gate or door ordained by God for me to possess today. All strength I need to accomplish God's will is released, and every lesson or discipline God wants me to endure will be learned.

"The LORD is my Rock. Praise the LORD! He prepares me for war. He trains me for battle" (Psalm 144:1 ERV).

Lord, confront every human and spiritual instrument of satanic persecution in our nation.

Every covering or veil resulting from the influence of idolatry over our nation is torn apart today.

Lord, I thank You for victory in every area of my life! I walk in favor, breakthrough, blessings and honor today and every day, in Jesus' name.

26. FOURTH WATCH OF THE DAY

3:00 P.M. TO 6:00 P.M.

C ommuning with God must be an integral part of every church. Prayer is among the most important privileges and distinctions of the Church. Although the Church is called to pray at all times, the only time of day in the Bible that is specifically referred to as the "hour of prayer" begins at 3:00 p.m.: "Now Peter and John went up together into the temple at the hour of prayer, being the ninth hour" (Acts 3:1).

DISTINCTIONS OF THIS WATCH: A TIME OF TRIUMPH

- The hour of prayer is a time to shape history. During this hour, Jesus declared, "It is finished," and, with a loud voice, gave up the ghost (that is, died) after six hours on the cross. In that instant, history was changed forever.

Now from the sixth hour there was darkness over all the land until the ninth hour. And about the ninth hour Jesus cried out with a loud voice, saying, "Eli, Eli, lama sabachthani?" that is to say, "My God, My God, why hast Thou forsaken Me?"...Jesus, when He had cried out again with a loud voice, yielded up the ghost.

MATTHEW 27:45–46, 50

- At the same moment, the veil in front of the holy of holies tore from top to bottom. This hour is a time to remove veils and limiting factors from your life.

> And behold, the veil of the temple was rent in two from the top to the bottom, and the earth quaked and the rocks rent.
>
> **MATTHEW 27:51**

- This watch is a time for divine ascension. Elijah mended the altar and prepared the sacrifice at this time. At the hour of prayer, he raised his voice and prayed.

> *And it came to pass, when midday was past, and they prophesied until the time of the offering of the evening sacrifice, that there was neither voice, nor any to answer, nor any that regarded. And Elijah said unto all the people, "Come near unto me." And all the people came near unto him. And he repaired the altar of the LORD that was broken down.*
>
> **1 KINGS 18:29–30**

- The hour of prayer is the hour of triumph, a time to see the Kingdom of God established in a new way. It is a time to die to the world (the self); God's agenda takes precedence over our agenda, and His way over our own.

PRAYERS, DECREES AND CONFESSIONS

I thank God for sending Jesus, my Redeemer and High Priest.

God, give me grace to turn my back on everything that does not please You.

I pray that every veil and covering that might hinder my prayer and success in Your throne room be exposed.

Give me throne room experiences. Let me encounter heaven in a new way.

I decree that my old life is finished: failure, disappointment, setback, every sin habit, every area of financial lack, sickness, infirmity, every place of instability, prayerlessness, lust, anger, resentment, gossip, doubt—all are finished!

All curses and bondages hindering me are finished.

Thank You that Jesus was despised and forsaken so I can become accepted in the Beloved.

While I was yet a sinner, Christ died for the ungodly. Jesus was condemned so I could be forgiven.

Jesus died so that I might have life and have it more abundantly.

Jesus was pierced for my transgressions.

Jesus was bruised for my iniquity.

Jesus was punished in order to give me peace with God.

Jesus was made a curse so that I could be a blessing.

Let the Church of Christ live up to the level of victory of Christ, who died and rose again.

Lord, raise levels of creativity so that the lesser known sports and arts that can build society are enhanced, while those that have brought ungodliness decrease.

Lord, I ask that You fan the flames of creative gifts that have been given to individuals in my family, church and nation. Let these giftings be honored in a new way in the school system, and let funding be provided for them.

I rebuke every evil reinforcement and dissolve every satanic network standing in the way of my retribution.

The devil departs for a season to regroup (Luke 4:13). I fortify myself with anointing through prayer, worship and praise against every sneak attack of the enemy.

I pray according to Isaiah 54:15: Behold, they shall surely gather together, but not by the Lord's hand; whosoever shall gather together against me shall fall. As the enemies of the Lord fall before Him, my enemies fall before me.

Let every organized strategy and assignment against my life initiated by demonic hosts be rendered to nothing.

I rebuke every demonic influence intended for destroying my vision, dream and ministry.

Let every demonic trap set against me be shattered to pieces.

I command all demonic activity against my calling to cease its work against me.

Lord, raise up intercessors to stand in the gap for me always.

Let all the motionless spiritual gifts and talents in my life begin to function for Your glory.

I reject all uncontrollable crying, heaviness and regret. I command every spirit of depression and mental illness to be turned. My mind and emotions are being healed now, in Jesus' name.

I command all organized forces of darkness against my life to be subjected to commotion and confusion. Let my enemies turn against each other.

I decree that every spiritual spider (assignments of witchcraft) building webs of problems in my life will die immediately.

I command every evil cycle in my life to break. I refuse to continue moving through unprofitable cycles, in Jesus' name.

I speak confusion over every evil confederacy forming evil counsel over my life and family.

I decree that my health will not waste my money.

I refuse to wear the garment of sorrow any longer. I receive the spirit of Kingdom praise!

I send back every evil arrow of business failure, contract delays and resource delays. I refuse to be defeated when I should be victorious.

I bind and render to nothing every strongman troubling my life. Let every threefold cord of wickedness operating against me be dismantled.

I decree that there shall be no reinforcement and no regrouping of any strongman against me.

Thank You, Lord, for answering my prayers.

God alone is to be worshiped, and I decree that all men will worship the Most High God. As the waters cover the sea, the whole earth will be filled with the knowledge of the glory of the Lord.

I ask the God of creation to place in me excellent creative abilities and open up creative ideas to me, so that in everything I do, I will be outstandingly creative and productive.

I ask for the kind of understanding that God alone can give, which no one can beat. Lord, I ask You today to release to me new levels of creativity and efficiency.

Lord, release the four winds and the breath of life, according to Ezekiel 37. Let us be filled with Your prophetic breath.

Everything that God meant to be alive but has died in my life, family, church, community and nation, I decree that life will be restored to it from the four winds of the earth. Let the breath of the Lord be released in my family, church, community and nation in a new way.

I pray that the scepter of God, which signifies the authority of the King, would be released in every area of society. Let the scepter of righteousness be released today.

I pray that Jehovah Elohim will take His rightful and sovereign place in society and that His rulership would be released in my family, church and nation.

I pray that Jehovah Elohim would exalt those who have humbled themselves under His authority and bring low every proud, exalted and arrogant thing in my life and nation.

Jehovah Elohim, begin to re-create my family life. Re-create and reorder the economies of my city and nation so that my nation can better submit and serve You.

Jehovah Elohim, You sit enthroned above the circle of the earth. Reduce and bring to nothing all Satan-inspired rulers in the nations, including those who have been entrenched or planted. God, I ask that You would uproot them according to Isaiah 40:21–24.

God, I ask that out of desolation, war, famine, poverty, malnutrition, instability, injustices and social and racial disparities, You would bring forth a new creation that will become a praise in the earth.

Lord, I ask that You would make Kingdom-oriented ministries a praise in the earth.

Lord, create in me a clean, pure, steadfast and obedient heart so that my worship will be acceptable unto You, according to Psalm 51 and Malachi 3:2–4.

I pray that You will cause me to feed on the living bread that comes down from heaven.

I am blessed (it is in my DNA) and I have a birthright (authority and inheritance).

I decree that the thrones in every pillar of society will follow after the throne of the Kingdom of God. I decree that honor, justice and righteousness will mark every throne of society.

No power of the moon will be used to destroy anything that belongs to my mind, marriage, family, business, health or church. God will keep me from all harm.

I decree the moon will mark seasons of prosperity, praise, righteousness, holiness and the power of God in my life.

I decree that those who worship the sun, moon and stars and instruct others to do the same will be judged. I decree revival among astrologers and soothsayers who use the sun, moon and stars for dark purposes.

I decree that leaders of nations will forsake and reject all advisors and aides who burn incense to the sun, moon and constellations.

I decree that the glory of the Lord and of the Lamb of God will be my light by night to show the way forward.

I decree an end to instability and turbulence in my life. I will not be tossed back and forth by every wind of doctrine, nor by the sleight and cunning of men or women who wait to deceive me.

I decree that the day will bring out the solid and stable aspects of my life, family, community and church.

I decree that I am immovable, steadfast and stable, and I abound in the work of the Lord.

I decree that I will not fall, I will not fear and I will not fail in life.

Lord, You are the Man of war. Scatter all the armies that have come to fight against me.

Lord, according to Psalm 35, contend with those who contend against me. Every day will be a fruitful day for me.

Lord establish every work of my hands today. Establish Kingdom-minded ministries in my territory, and establish Your Kingdom patterns in every pillar of society.

Lord, show me how to strengthen any areas of instability in my life and church.

Lord, arise and overthrow every modern-day Pharaoh in my nation, along with his chariots.

I decree victory in every area of my life, today and every day. I overcome every enemy by the blood of the Lamb!

NOTES

_____

_____

_____

_____

_____

_____

_____

_____

_____

_____

_____

_____

_____

_____

_____

_____

_____

_____

_____

CONFESSIONS

As you press toward victory, seeing more of your prayers answered, it is important to walk in joy. As you find time to declare these Scriptures each day, let the wells of joy deepen within you, flowing forth like a mighty river!

But let all those that put their trust in Thee rejoice; let them ever shout for joy, because Thou defendest them; let them also that love Thy name be joyful in Thee.

PSALM 5:11

Thou wilt show me the path of life; in Thy presence is fullness of joy; at Thy right hand there are pleasures for evermore.

PSALM 16:11

And then shall mine head be lifted up above mine enemies round about me; therefore I will offer in His tabernacle sacrifices of joy; I will sing, yea, I will sing praises unto the LORD.

PSALM 27:6

Let them shout for joy and be glad that favor my righteous cause; yea, let them say continually, "Let the LORD be magnified who hath pleasure in the prosperity of His servant."

PSALM 35:27

Restore unto me the joy of Thy salvation, and uphold me with Thy free Spirit.

PSALM 51:12

O come, let us sing unto the LORD! Let us make a joyful noise to the rock of our salvation!

PSALM 95:1

The LORD is my strength and my shield; my heart trusted in Him, and I am helped. Therefore my heart greatly rejoiceth, and with my song will I praise Him.

PSALM 28:7

I will call upon the LORD, who is worthy to be praised; so shall I be saved from mine enemies.

PSALM 18:3

Make a joyful noise unto the LORD, all ye lands! Serve the LORD with gladness; come before His presence with singing! Know ye that the LORD, He is God; it is He that hath made us, and not we ourselves. We are His people, and the sheep of His pasture. Enter into His gates with thanksgiving, and into His courts with praise! Be thankful unto Him, and bless His name! For the LORD is good, His mercy is everlasting; and His truth endureth to all generations.

PSALM 100

That ye might walk worthy of the Lord, in all pleasing Him, being fruitful in every good work, and increasing in the knowledge of God; strengthened with all might according to His glorious power, unto all patience and longsuffering with joyfulness; giving thanks unto the Father, who hath made us meet to be partakers of the inheritance of the saints in light.

COLOSSIANS 1:10–12

Now unto Him that is able to keep you from falling, and to present you faultless before the presence of His glory with exceeding joy...

JUDE 24

Praise ye the LORD! Praise the LORD, O my soul! While I live will I praise the LORD; I will sing praises unto my God while I have any being. Put not your trust in princes, nor in a son of man in whom there is no help. His breath goeth forth, he returneth to his earth; in that very day his thoughts perish. Happy is he that hath the God of Jacob for his help, whose hope is in the LORD his God, who made heaven and earth, the sea and all that therein is, who keepeth truth for ever; who executeth judgment for the oppressed, who giveth food to the hungry; the LORD looseth the prisoners. The LORD openeth the eyes of the blind; the LORD raiseth them that are bowed down; the LORD loveth the righteous. The LORD preserveth the strangers, He relieveth the fatherless and the widow; but the way of the wicked He turneth upside down. The LORD shall reign for ever, even Thy God, O Zion, unto all generations. Praise ye the LORD!

PSALM 146

Dr. Alston's Booking Information

Website:
www.drvjalston.org

E-mail:
info@drvjalston.org

Mailing Address:
10936 N. Port Washington Road Suite 226* Mequon, WI 53092

Resources

- Next-Level Spiritual Warfare:
  Advance Strategies for Defeating the Enemy

Available Regional Trainings

- School of Prayer and Spiritual Warfare
- School of the Prophets
- School of Global Leadership

ABOUT THE AUTHOR

The Kingdom of God is her heartbeat and preparing Christian leaders for maximum effectiveness, her passion. Dr. Venner Alston is the divine response to your hunger to experience a greater degree of excellence, in life and ministry. To the challenges your leaders and teams face, she brings her expertise in the areas of Team and Executive Coaching coupled with Church Administration and Education to design the effective, practical approaches that advance leaders and teams to the level of success every visionary organization desires. A prolific and penetrating speaker, teacher and life - coach, Dr. Alston provides radical strategies and cutting - edge methods to the many dilemmas that keep your leaders and teams stuck in ineffective paradigms.

Leveraging more than 25 years of global experience in developing and strengthening leaders and teams, with her undergraduate and graduate degrees in Education, Theology and a PhD in Urban Education, Dr. Alston is devoted to increasing your leadership and team effectiveness. She is the relevant answer you have been seeking to lead your organization to the productive of your dreams. She motivates your leaders and teams through speaking, coaching, leading executive or leadership retreats, conferences, workshops or one -on- one Executive Coaching sessions.

Dr. Venner Alston is available to provide the radical strategies and cutting-edge approaches that inspire and empower Kingdom leaders and teams produce lasting results. We look forward to assisting you meet your growth and transformation needs in the near future.

Printed in the USA
CPSIA information can be obtained
at www.ICGtesting.com
LVHW011251310823
756864LV00007B/224